easy to grow!
Pots & Containers

Good Housekeeping

easy to grow!
Pots &
Containers

COLLINS & BROWN

First published in the United Kingdom in 2010 by
Collins & Brown
10 Southcombe Street
London
W14 0RA

An imprint of Anova Books Company Ltd

The Good Housekeeping website is
www.allboutyou.com/goodhousekeeping

10 9 8 7 6 5 4 3 2 1

ISBN 978-1-84340-541-2
A catalogue record for this book is available from the
British Library.

Reproduction by Dot Gradations Ltd, UK
Printed and bound by Times Offset, Malaysia

This book can be ordered direct from the publisher at
www.anovabooks.com

The following pictures are reproduced with kind permission of GAP
picture library and John Glover, Lynn Keddie, Graham Strong, Sarah
Cuttle, Friderich Strauss, Brian North, Clive Nichols, JS Sira, Mel
Watson, Jerry Harpur, Ron Evans, Jonathan Buckley, Jo Whitworth,
Leigh Clapp, Richard Bloom, Neil Holmes, S&O, and Rob Whitworth:
P.13; P.14 (R); P.15; P.23 (L); P.24 (L,R); P.25; P.27; P.38; P.41;
P.44; P.83 (R); P.97 (L); P.98; P.109 (R); P.111 (L); P.112; P.115;
P.116; P.117; P.118; P.119; P.120; P.121; P.122 (L,R); P.123.

Colour photography by Lucinda Symons on the following pages:
P.30 (L,R); P.31 (L,R); P.32 (L,R); P.34; P.36 (L,R); P.40; P.42;
P.43 (all).

The Publisher would like to thank Ginkgo Gardens for the kind use
of their centre.

The publication is designed to provide accurate and authoritative
information in regard to the subject matter covered. It is sold on
the understanding that the Publishers is not engaged in rendering
professional services. If professional advice or other expert
assistance is required, the services of a competent professional
should be sought.

Contents

Basics

Tools and materials

Before you get started on gardening with pots and containers, you are going to need a basic set of tools. Always buy the best you can afford. Saving money on tools is a false economy. Choose those made from stainless steel with solid wood handles. Never buy unseen, try them out for size and comfort first.

It will make a big difference to your workload if your tools are comfortable to use. Take good care of them, as well. Clean off mud and soil after use and wipe them over with a cloth before putting them away. Service them regularly and sharpen them as necessary and they will last you for years.

Basic set

Spade: Needed for moving soil and compost into larger pots and containers. They come in many different sizes and shapes, which is why you need to try them to find the one that suits you best. Make sure that the tread on the shoulders fits your foot comfortably, as well.

Hand trowel and fork: The trowel is a versatile tool, but is primarily used for planting. The fork is useful for weeding near plants and loosening soil. They need to be sturdy and well made. They come in different shapes and sizes, so take your time to find the one that is most comfortable for you.

Pocket knife: Invaluable for slitting open bags of compost or manure, cutting twine, taking cuttings, etc.

Sharpening stone: Useful to have to keep edges sharp and well maintained.

Secateurs/shears: For pruning, cutting, deadheading, keeping things tidy.

Others

Watering can: Chose a sturdy one – plastic or metal – with a capacity of seven to nine litres (1½–2 gallons). You will need two detachable roses – one coarse and one fine – so you can match flow to plant.

Wheelbarrow: For moving large bags of compost, manure, plants, bags, etc. Again, size and balance is personal and you may find a secondhand one does the job as well.

Bucket: For holding compost and liquid materials.

Riddle: For sieving compost.

Carrying sheet or bag: Keep nearby while working to save time on trips to the compost heap or shed.

Bamboo canes: A selection of various sizes for marking out areas or positions, and providing support for plants, nets and wire.

Twine: For tying up branches, stems, canes, wires, etc.

Gloves: Choose a lighter, supple pair for pruning and planting, and a heavy duty pair for messier jobs such as handling prickly and stinging plants.

Horticultural fleece: To protect plants from the cold or pests, or to warm up the ground.

Cloches: A variety of different shapes, sizes and materials, including glass, plastic and polyurethane. For covering rows or individual plants – useful if you want to bring forward or extend the growing season, or for warming up the soil prior to sowing or planting.

Cold frames: Used for bringing on young plants or protecting a growing crop. They can be static with a solid floor, or movable (without a floor) to offer protection for plants growing in the ground, or adapted to make a hot bed.

For sowing seeds

Seed trays and small pots: Made of plastic (though wooden and terracotta types are also available) and used for sowing seeds that need to be pricked out when they have germinated.

Modules: For sowing individual seeds to grow on to the planting out stage.

Hand tools
Good quality hand tools with solid wood handles will last longer and make container gardening much easier.

Biodegradable pots: Used for sowing crops that do not like their roots disturbed. Once the seedling is large enough to be planted out in the ground, the whole thing can go in and the container will rot down as the plant grows.

Dibber: A pointed metal or wood tool used to make holes for planting seeds or young plants. A small one is essential for pricking out seedlings.

Labels and marker: Essential so you know what is where. Many different types available in plastic, wood or slate with appropriate pencil or pen.

Propagator lids: Usually made of clear plastic and put over seed trays to speed up germination. You could also use cut-off plastic bottles set over individual pots.

Electric propagator: A small unit in which seeds are placed when a specific temperature is needed to germinate them (usually 13–16°C/55–61°F). The heat source may be a light bulb, heated plates or coils. Not essential, but a useful piece of equipment to have and they are usually inexpensive to run.

Choosing pots and containers

The most important thing when choosing containers is to ensure that they fit in with their surroundings. Another is cost – handmade terracotta is expensive, but a search of junk or antique shops may produce worthwhile trophies for little money. Whatever style of pots you choose, make sure that they will look good together and will complement the overall style of your garden.

If you plan an extensive container garden, then you will need containers of various shapes and sizes for large and small plants. If they are to be grouped then the groupings must match. One of the most popular materials is terracotta, with pots available in many shapes and sizes. Many of the designs are copies of Victorian styles which were available in the 19th century, and some of the more elaborate urns are based on classical designs. If you do not like the rather raw orange-brown colour of new cheap pots, you can tone them down by painting them in soft colours. Alternatively, encourage them to 'age' more quickly by painting them in yogurt or a mixture of sour milk and yogurt; this attracts algae, and within just a few weeks will give the pot a pleasant greenish patina.

Troughs and basins

A container garden which contained only pots would look rather dull and consequently it is worthwhile incorporating a number of troughs as well. The most expensive and heaviest of these are made from lead but there are now many designs manufactured from fibreglass or stone. You could also use kitchen sinks and stone troughs.

Always position large pots, urns and troughs before filling and planting them; once full, they may be too heavy to move. Place the empty pots where you think you would like them to go, then move them around before you fill them up, trying out different arrangements until you are satisfied they fit the space and look good in your chosen locations.

Groupings of containers
They don't have to be all of the same material but containers will look better together if you keep to the same look – either traditional or modern.

Most containers are made from terracotta, literally 'baked earth'. New pots can be painted or aged to look good in any area.

WHAT TO CHOOSE

There is a wide variety of containers available. Here are some tips to help you choose what is best for you.

If you are clustering pots together, choose different sizes for as much variety as possible.

Look for frost-resistant labels on terracotta pots. These will withstand cold winters.

Terracotta pots come in lovely shapes, but choose a wider neck for greater plant accessibility.

Terracotta containers make great windowboxes, but check them for fit before you buy.

A low, wide container is perfect for displaying low-growing plants such as sedums.

Reconstituted stone containers look very realistic and are a fraction of the cost of those made from carved stone.

Fake lead pots look very much like the real thing but are much lighter and easier to handle. They are also a great deal less expensive to buy.

Wall pots

Container gardens can be extended upwards to great effect using wall pots. These can be planted to create a range of interesting effects.

The container gardener can extend the number of plants and the growing area by using a variety of wall pots attached to available walls and pergolas. These are especially useful for planting up balconies where it is unlikely that there will be room for raised beds to accommodate climbers to cover walls or trellises.

Using wall pots

The most attractive wall pots are made in terracotta with flat backs. They come in various shapes and designs and groups of these can be positioned on a wall, planted to paint an abstract picture. These can be filled with flowers, herbs or vegetables, such as French beans, or better still trailing tomatoes that will hang over the edge of the pot. They are not suitable for all plants, and planning and planting must be undertaken with care. If they are used for vegetables they must be placed low enough so that the leaves and fruit can be harvested easily. This position also assists watering and it is an important point that wall pots must be easily watered either by watering can or by a hose with a long-armed attachment.

Homemade containers – windowboxes and troughs

It is frequently difficult to find containers to fit a particular space. Windowsills may be too large, or too small for the boxes you can buy: balconies may require larger boxes than those you can find if the overall design is to be maintained, or you may not like the design of the individual planters available. One solution is to make your own containers. A range of containers can be made quite simply from pressure-treated wood or marine ply. Line the containers in thick plastic (with holes for drainage), to extend their life and to keep any wood treatments away from the plants.

You can also make a number of wooden containers, such as troughs and Versailles tubs, in various shapes and designs that fit the style of the garden.

Wooden boxes

There are many good books available that give advice on constructing windowboxes and troughs for the garden. The projects vary in complexity and the number of tools that are required.

Measure everything carefully. Use substantial, thick wood or MDF board. It should be at least 19mm (¾in) thick. Make sure that the corners and bottom are properly secured. Either buy a routing tool that enables

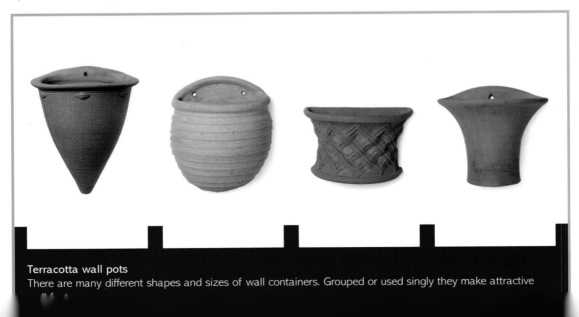

Terracotta wall pots
There are many different shapes and sizes of wall containers. Grouped or used singly they make attractive

A summer-flowering windowbox with shades of purple and silver looks good from both inside and outside the house.

you to make grooved joints or secure the sides and bottom to battens so that the box is rigid and firm.

Check the design

Make sure that the windowbox fits in well with the window it accompanies and looks right when it is in position. This also applies to planters that stand on their own on patios or balconies, such as Versailles tubs or wooden boxes. You should treat all wood with horticulturally recommended preservative, following the instructions on the label, and paying particular attention to the cut edges of the windowbox. Drill holes in the base to allow the container to drain and line it with thick polythene that can be stapled in place with a staple gun. Make drainage holes in the polythene and check that these align with the holes in the base of the container.

Containers for indoor use

When selecting pots and containers for use indoors, always think carefully about the decor of the rooms in which they will be positioned. For aesthetic reasons, it is important to buy decorative containers that will not only match well with the plants they are to hold but also with the fixtures and fittings that surround them.

Just as with outdoor container gardening, there is really no limit to the types, sizes and styles of pots and containers that you can use to decorate your home. The golden rule is that the containers always enhance rather than clash with your interior design.

In order not to damage furniture and carpets when indoor containers are being watered or topped up with growing medium, place saucers, dinner plates or cache pots beneath the receptacles.

Unusual containers

Painted old car tyres make unusual containers for all plants and are much used for planting potatoes. Add a base to the lowest tyre, ensuring that there is sufficient drainage, then pile the others on top.

Choosing containers – larger plants

There are a number of things to think about when considering larger plants. Many trees and shrubs will need as big a container as you can provide, if they are to flourish and attain anywhere near their potential proportions.

Larger plants are best grown in raised beds or in special containers chosen so that they fit in with the overall design of the garden. Even big containers need to have drainage at the bottom and an automatic watering system is of great assistance in keeping the plants moist.

Match the container to the plant

Try to match the style of the container to the style of the plant. Trees or shrubs with a spreading habit look best in wide-brimmed pots. Very often large containers are made from terracotta, but other materials, such as stone or glazed earthenware, are also suitable, provided they can accommodate the root system of the plant. Keep the containers and their contents in proportion. It is always possible to pot on a tree as it grows into a larger container, and any small plant alone in a large pot will look bare and isolated. It is best to fill in the space around the main plant with low-growing plants, as this will keep the planting in proportion.

Barrels and tall pots

Half barrels make good containers and can accommodate quite large trees. They look natural and will fit in with almost any surrounding. You may be able to find old barrels in a junk shop or scrap yard, or ask at your local brewery.

Tall pots sometimes make excellent features on a patio garden. Ali Baba pots are very decorative on their own and hardly need to be filled with plants. A good tip for planting an Ali Baba type pot or a chimney or very big pot is to put a small pot or basket in the top and just fill that with soil – rather than filling the entire chimney with soil. If you are planning to plant up a very tall pot, be careful. There are few plants that work well in really big containers. Choose some trailing nasturtiums or something equally simple.

Very large containers need to be placed carefully in the garden and particular care has to be taken over the background. The design of a garden is composed of many things, but the background colour is very often forgotten.

Large containers
Bigger plants are needed to complement the proportions of larger containers such as half barrels and tall urns.

Chimney pots make striking containers of different heights. You can buy them in some antique shops and

Choosing plants

For both indoors and outdoors container gardening, make a list of all the plants that you want to grow in your various pots and containers and stick to it. Remember that plants get bigger; don't worry if the containers look a bit bare when first planted, they will soon fill out. On the other hand, match your plants carefully to your containers. You don't want to choose plants that will massively outgrow the pots within a few years, any more than you want plants that are too small.

The most important thing to consider when growing any plant in a container is the direction of the sun. In the northern hemisphere, if a patio faces south, it is sheltered, and if the general climate is hot enough, heat-loving plants can be grown. If the patio faces north, then you should concentrate on those plants that will flourish in a degree of shade.

It is important to plan purchasing and planting carefully. Make a list of the plants that you plan to grow then check whether there is a specialist nursery near you. If there is, you can purchase the plants you require in person, but you may have to order them to be sent by mail. Nurseries are well used to sending plants through the post and it is seldom that plants arrive in anything other than good condition. It is best to buy from a specialist, rather than from a general garden centre or supermarket where the choice may be limited and, usually, no specialist advice or help is available.

Planting at the right time

Plants should be planted at the right time of the year and this applies particularly to trees and shrubs. Generally these are always best planted in the autumn when the growth is dying down but there remains enough warmth and moisture in the soil to let the root system establish itself.

Plants that have been raised in containers often have a restricted root system and bare-root plants planted at the right time of the year do better. No reputable supplier would send out bare-root plants at the wrong time of the year.

If you cannot plant any trees or shrubs as soon as they arrive, dig a small trench in one container, lay the plants in it at an angle of 45 degrees and cover them firmly with soil until you have time to complete the planting properly. The plants are unlikely to come to too much harm if they are not left for too long. If a frost threatens, protect them by covering them with garden fleece or some sacking.

Other plants may be suitable only for very particular times of year – such as summer bedding plants like dahlias and more exotic, tender species such as cannas, lantana and felicia. These can all be planted in succession with spring bulbs, evergreens, ornamental grasses, bamboos and so on, in order to provide your containers with spectacular year-round displays.

Buying plants at a nursery

If you plan to buy the plants yourself at a garden centre – whether for outdoor or indoor use – there are a number of things to look out for. Check all the leaves for signs of pests or disease, and make sure that the plant does not suffer from leaf drop. Avoid plants that have moss growing on the top of the container, as this indicates that they have been there for too long. Check to see that there are not too many roots growing out of the holes at the foot of the container for the same reason.

Finally, check to see that the plant is healthy and that it has a good shape with equally spaced branches, fronds or leaves. Remember that you may want to turn containers round so that each plant gets an equal share of the light over the year.

This is an excellent example of achieving different levels on a patio with a variety of containers, large and

Unsuitable plants for pots and containers

Plants with short flowering seasons, a straggly growth habit, uninteresting foliage, tall gangly stems or only one feature of interest instead of several, generally make unexciting subjects for containers. Some plants need putting into soil or compost soon after you buy them, as they quickly spoil if they are allowed to dry out at the roots. Other plants are unsuitable for long-term growing in containers because they get too big or grow so vigorously that they soon exhaust the limited amount of potting mixture, even in a large container. This is particularly true of climbing roses, cane fruits and large climbers. However, do not be put off using shade- and moisture-loving plants – many of them make good container plants, given the right conditions.

Plants to avoid

Avoid plants that cause skin reactions, such as rue and some primulas. Containers are often placed where people brush against them.

Plants that dislike being moved. All container plants need repotting every few years to give them fresh soil, so avoid species that do not respond well to this, such as hellebores and euphorbias.

Large untidy or fast-growing shrubs and conifers soon outgrow their containers.

Variegated weeping fig and other tropical foliage plants are easily spoiled by lack of proper care indoors.

Huge, fast-growing herbs, such as angelica, soon smother other herbs in a tub.

Most conifers go brown if they dry out at the roots and the foliage remains brown.

Large trees, including woodland and forest species, are unsuitable for containers unless you train them as bonsai specimens.

Large ornamental trees become potbound and dry out faster than you can water them.

BUILDING A RAISED BED

If you have a larger patio, you may want to build some raised beds. These allow you to grow larger and more substantial plants, such as fruit trees and shrubs. Raised beds can be built out of brick or breeze block that can then be rendered and painted.

1 Mark out the area with string and dig a trench 30cm (12in) wide and 30cm (12in) deep. Fill this footing with concrete.

2 When the concrete has dried, build the inner wall using breeze blocks. Lay each block on a 12mm (½in) layer of mortar. Check for level.

3 Build the outer brick walls out from each corner. Set a string guideline between the corners and insert metal wall ties at intervals.

4 Lay a top layer of bricks lengthways across both the inner and outer walls. Fill the base with drainage material and compost on top.

Plants for indoors

Plants would not naturally choose to live indoors, where the air is dry, the growing area is severely restricted, and supplies of water are limited. In fact, it is amazing that some plants survive indoors at all – yet they do. Many plants often survive periods spent in less-than-ideal conditions without suffering too much damage, but they will not thrive as well as they would in a situation that is perfectly suited to their needs.

Locating house plants

The worst places in the house, in terms of plants, are in direct heat, deep shade, or strong air currents. Not many plants can tolerate being on a windowsill facing the sun in summer, when the intensity of the heat can wilt the plant and scorch the leaves.

In deeply shaded parts of the house, light levels are not sufficient to allow photosynthesis to take place, denying the plant the carbohydrates it needs to live. In a draughty position, a lack of humidity will cause the leaves of more delicate plants to turn brown and wilt.

Plants for shady places

Flowering houseplants do not thrive in the more shady areas of the home because they need maximum light in order to mature and produce flower buds. For this situation, choose foliage plants with mid- to dark green leaves, because they can cope with low light.

Keep in mind that nothing will grow where the light level is very low because the plant will be unable to photosynthesize. Avoid white- or yellow-leaf variegations. The colour will be lost as the plant attempts to adapt to the more shady surroundings – there is no chlorophyll in the variegated part of the leaf, reducing the plant's ability to produce food. Look for plants with leathery or waxy dark green leaves. The darker green they are, the better the plant will tolerate the lack of light. The following indoor container plants will all do well in shady locations.

Plants for shady places

Aspidistra elatior
Asplenium nidus
x *Fatshedera lizei*
Howea forsteriana
Maranta leuconeura
Monstera deliciosa
Nephrolepsis exaltata 'Bostoniensis'
Philodendron bipinnatifidum
Saxifraga stolonifera
Senecio macroglossus

Aspidistras were the favourites of the Victorians, as one of the few houseplants that could survive in their shady parlours.

Tender geraniums (pelargoniums) will provide flowers and fill the room with scent.

Plants for a sunny room

A sunny room would seem to be the ideal spot for most plants, with plenty of light and warmth, but as with any other location, you still need to make sure that you are putting the right plant in the right place.

Most indoor plants will thrive as long as they are not in direct scorching sun, particularly at midday. The bright, hot sun, intensified by window glass, will cause sap inside the leaves to overheat and damage the cells, leading to scorching. Desert cacti can usually tolerate a sunny windowsill, as can seasonal pot plants when the heat is less intense, such as spring bulbs and flowering plants. Other plants will be happy for most of the day, but may need a little protection when the sun is at its highest.

Plants for a sunny room

Aloe vera

Clivia miniata

Grevillea robusta

Nerium oleander

Passiflora caerulea

Pelargonium spp.

Pentas lanceolata

Plumbago auriculata

Rose chinensis – Miniature roses

Sansevieria trifasciata

Stephanotis floribunda

Thunbergia alata

Plants for the hallway

The porch, entrance hallway or corridor may be bright or shady, but they share the common problem of being prone to draughts. Sudden changes in temperature as well as rapid changes in humidity can affect many plants.

Most plants grow best where the conditions change very little on a day-to-day basis. For porches, hallways or corridors you will need to look for tolerant flowering and foliage plants (to suit the available light levels) that will not mind the fluctuating temperatures and conditions.

When looking for a suitable place to site your plants in these locations, make sure that they will not be in a position where they will be continually brushed up against by people walking past. Flowering plants can easily have their blooms knocked off, and the leaves of foliage plants can become battered and browned at the edges, which can eventually impede their growth. Place on a pedestal table or on a ledge, if there is one in the hallway.

Plants for the hallway

Campanula isophylla
Cyclamen persicum
x *Fatshedera lizei*
Hedera helix
Impatiens spp.
Narcissus spp.
Pelargonium spp.
Rosa miniature
Saxifraga stolonifera
Thunbergia alata
Tolmeia menziesii
Tradescantia spp.

Cyclamen are tolerant of changes in conditions but do need plenty of light in order to flower well.

Achimenes will love high humidity in the bathroom but need to be kept in moist compost at all times.

Bougainvillea is a climber with vibrant coloured flowers – ideal for a very sunny spot.

Plants for the bathroom

The atmosphere in the bathroom tends to vary widely from hot and steamy when it is in use, to cool and drier when it is not. The steam means that the humidity level is higher than elsewhere in the house, but the plant needs to be able to withstand the fluctuating temperatures.

Ferns are a good choice for this environment, as long as the temperature does not drop too low, as are dramatic foliage plants and tolerant species such as the spider plant.

Bathrooms are ideal for these plants, and the environment will prevent foliage from turning brown at the edges – which happens if they are kept in positions without high humidity. Position in groups of the same plant or have a variety of different plants.

Plants for the bathroom

Achimenes spp.
Adiantum spp.
Asparagus densiflorus 'Sprengeri'
Begonia spp.
Dracaena cvs.
Exacum affine
Gardenia augusta
Impatiens New Guinea hybrids
Nephrolepsis exaltata
Peperomia spp.
Pteris cretica

Plants for garden rooms

Conservatories, sunrooms and terraces offer a range of growing conditions, all different from those found inside the home. These rooms and spaces provide excellent places to sit and enjoy your plants, almost as if you were sitting in the garden.

The higher light levels in these locations mean that plants will grow well. However, scorch may be a problem on susceptible plants unless shade can be provided from the most intense sun around midday. Draughts can be more of a problem here than indoors, so choose plants that are tolerant of the conditions or that enjoy a period outdoors in summer. The more protected the situation, the greater the range of plants that can be grown. Make the best of the surroundings and use specimen plants to make a serious impact.

Plants for garden rooms

Allamanda cathartica
Argyranthemum cvs.
Bougainvillea glabra
Dracaena cvs.
Fatsia japonica
Nerium oleander
Pentas lanceolata
Plumbago auriculata
Primula obconica
Rhododendron simsii
Thunbergia alata

Hanging baskets

Hanging baskets are especially useful for placing on balconies or to cover walls or trellises. Once lined and planted they can look most attractive. Planting hanging baskets is not nearly as difficult as it might appear. They should be planted in late spring, although they need protection overnight if there is any threat of frost.

Liner options

Traditional wire hanging baskets must be lined before use. Moss-lined baskets look spectacular, as the wire framework allows you to plant the sides and base of the basket as well as the top, but they drip when watered and dry out quickly. Modern, solid-sided hanging baskets are easier to look after, but you cannot plant the sides. For the best of both worlds, use one of the modern liners inside a traditional basket.

Solid baskets

Baskets with solid sides include plastic and self-watering types as well as plastic-lined wicker baskets, which now come in a range of novel shapes, including the cornucopia and cone. These are simple to plant up, though rarely as luxuriant as open-sided baskets which allow a wider variety of plants to be used.

Large solid baskets do have the advantage of not drying out as quickly, especially ones containing a self-watering reservoir. These have a base covered with capillary matting below the compost and plants, and a wick that extends from that and dips into the reservoir. There are seep holes at the top of the reservoir so that excess water can drain away and more sophisticated models usually have a watering tube which directs water straight into the compartment. If you follow the manufacturer's instructions, once a good root system has established, you should be able to leave the basket unattended for a couple of days.

A conical basket allows planting at the top but not in its sides.

A traditional basket like this is perfect for a reservoir. Even an old saucer placed inside the basket will capture some of the water and hold it for the plants.

For a full display like this, plants need to be positioned all around the sides of the basket as well as in the top of the compost.

Designing with containers

All successful gardens fulfil a purpose. They please the eye and provide a blend of colour and shape to enhance the beauty of the house they surround. This is as true for a container garden as it is for any garden with a large formal design. Container gardens are usually planned and planted on a small scale and great care has to be taken with each component so that the perfect blend is achieved.

Using the available space

Even the smallest patio garden should not reveal its secrets all at once. Plan the positioning of the containers so that you have to walk in curves and round corners to find out what comes next.

The first thing any gardener has to do when planning a garden is to measure the space there is available. This is particularly important when planning a kitchen container garden, as when space is limited greater care has to be taken to make sure every bit is used to the best advantage.

Whether the space is large or small two fundamental rules apply: all the elements of the garden must be easily reachable, and there must be a clear plan to the area. These may seem too elementary, even unnecessary, but planning involves simple things, such as allowing space to walk out of the back door, making sure you can reach all the containers to water them, allowing access to an outside tap, and checking the position of any windows so that growing plants will not obstruct the light. It is surprising how often such practicalities are forgotten.

If your container garden is a windowbox or on a small balcony, then there is usually little choice about how the space can be organized and used.

If the container garden is on a patio or roof garden then you have to think about all the likely uses for the space. Is it used for eating out in the summer or sunbathing? Is it an extra room? Do the family sit there? How much competition for the space is there between the gardening and non-gardening members of the family?

Raised beds and potagers

Once these questions have been answered you can decide, for instance, whether there is room for a raised bed around a patio area or whether the patio is large enough to create a miniature potager kitchen garden with small formal beds of herbs and vegetables.

Raised beds have a number of advantages: they are more easily reached by the elderly and disabled; they provide a garden with the large containers that are necessary if permanent trees and shrubs are to be grown; and they give a container garden more substance. If you plan to build one, remember to allow space between the container and the walls of the house, as otherwise the damp course would be compromised.

Pay attention to the design and think carefully about the final result before you start. There may be room for small, free-standing beds in the middle of a terrace or roof garden that allow all-round access, and two small beds may look better than one large one.

Similarly, if you want to construct a potager, take care not to interfere with the drains or mains supplies to the house or flat.

The vertical dimension

Height and different levels are another important consideration. Are you surrounded by a wall or trellis? Can you position containers so that you can grow climbing plants that will screen you from view? Is there sufficient wall space to grow trees and shrubs? Have you got walls that will support wall pots? Might it be possible to plan arches or pergolas to cover a seating area with vines or other climbing plants? Two essential points in all garden design are access and surprise. Try and achieve a dynamic practical flow, that carries you around the area, however small.

Aims and objectives

Even small gardens must have form and colour. Organize the containers into a pleasing, coherent pattern and grow plants with different shades of leaf colour throughout the year.

When you have finished planning out the space, you can start to implement the design. Draw the garden to scale on a piece of graph paper, putting in all the essential features, such as doors, windows, walls, fences and taps. Then transfer this design on to the ground, marking out the areas you have chosen for containers in chalk on the patio, or cut out sheets of paper to match the shapes of the containers. See whether this makes sense. Walk round them and change their position until you are completely satisfied. It is always possible to move containers but it is irksome to realize that a permanent feature such as a raised bed is not in the right place when you have spent money and effort building it.

Aspect

This is an important consideration for any patio gardener and it is the one thing that cannot be changed. Check which direction your garden faces and assess how much sun it gets each day.

There is absolutely no point whatsoever trying to grow herbs from the Mediterranean, that by their very nature like heat and sun, if all you can offer them is a shady, north-facing patio. This is the basic rule for all gardens, disheartening or not, but if you read the conditions that each plant prefers before planning, buying and planting you will avoid considerable disappointment and also save money.

Planning displays indoors

Many of the same principles apply to arranging groups of container plants indoors. Indeed, it is even more important to ensure that light conditions and the temperature are suitable for your indoor pot plants, as they will be growing in what is essentially an artificial environment. With regard to the containers themselves, ensure that they are of similar styles and sizes, with no one pot overly dominating the display.

Matching pots of lavender echo the lavender hedge of a formal garden. Here the containers have been arranged so that they can be brushed against, making the beautiful scent even more immediate.

Choosing the growing medium

There are three groups of compost and a number of special composts for different plants. For general container gardening, sowing seeds or planting, a good, multi-purpose compost is best.

Seed composts are specifically formulated for growing seeds. They may be loam-based (that is, contain soil) or be peat- or peat-substitute-based. They contain few nutrients, they are very fine so that the seed has close contact with the compost and they retain water well. If seedlings are kept in seed compost for any length of time after germination before pricking out, they will need additional feeding.

Multi-purpose composts

These can be used to germinate seedlings and also to pot up a number of plants. They fall in between seed compost and potting compost. If you are going to use multi-purpose for pots then you will need to feed rather more than if you used a normal potting compost, but this is only a minor consideration. These are probably the best composts to buy for general garden work, but they should not be used for containers with large permanent plants.

Potting composts

Composts are either loam-based or peat-based. Loam-based composts are all based on the John Innes formulae. They retain water and nutrients better than peat-based composts and are more suitable for long-term growth. John Innes No 3 contains three times more nutrients than John Innes No 1 and is the best compost for established plants and trees.

Peat-based compost (including peat substitutes such as coir) is more readily available, lighter, cleaner and easier to work with. Use it for general gardening in smaller containers.

Special composts

A number of special potting composts are available, including ericaceous compost for acid-loving plants, orchid compost, alpine and cacti composts, bulb fibre compost, and hanging basket compost that contains water-retaining granules.

If you live in an area where the soil is very alkaline, you can grow acid-loving plants in containers rather than in your unsuitable garden soil. This applies more to flowers and shrubs, such as camellias and rhododendrons, than it does to fruit and vegetables, but some fruit must be grown in ericaceous compost.

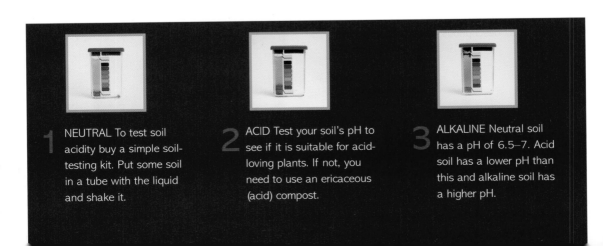

1 NEUTRAL To test soil acidity buy a simple soil-testing kit. Put some soil in a tube with the liquid and shake it.

2 ACID Test your soil's pH to see if it is suitable for acid-loving plants. If not, you need to use an ericaceous (acid) compost.

3 ALKALINE Neutral soil has a pH of 6.5–7. Acid soil has a lower pH than this and alkaline soil has a higher pH.

Weeding

Weeds compete directly with your container plants for light, nutrients and water. They can also act as hosts to pests and diseases (see pages 46–7), which can spread as the season progresses. Groundsel, for instance, often harbours the fungal diseases rust and mildew, and sap-sucking aphids. Chickweed also plays host to aphids as well as red spider mites.

Annual weeds

Clearing annual weeds in containers by hand is quick and effective, but the timing is important. The weeding must be done when the weeds are tiny and before they start producing seed.

Breaking the tops off container weeds will sever the stems of young weeds from the root system just below soil level. This both prevents the stem from forming new roots and stops the roots from producing a new stem.

There is an old saying, 'One year's seeds make seven years' weeds', which has now been endorsed by scientific research and proved to be remarkably accurate – unfortunately for gardeners.

Annual weeds are capable of producing a staggering total of 60,000 viable seeds per square yard, per year. The vast majority of these seeds are found in the uppermost 5cm (2in) of soil, but they will usually germinate only when exposed to sufficient light levels. This is why mulching (see pages 38–9), which covers the soil and blocks out light, has become such a widely popular method of weed control, both in the garden at large and in pots and containers of all descriptions. The added benefit of mulching is that there is also little chance of contaminating the soil with chemical residue.

Weeds will take hold in the soil or compost of larger container plants such as this Aspidistra unless regular maintenance is undertaken.

Potting and re-potting plants

The principles of planting and repotting are the same. Plants need to be firm in the compost to prevent air pockets around their roots and have adequate drainage to avoid waterlogging.

All plants grown in containers should be planted the same way. Choose a container 5cm (2in) larger than the rootball of the plant. Remove the plant from the original container and gently tease out the roots if they have become congested. Trim off any damaged roots. Put a good layer of crocks, broken tiles or stones at the bottom of the container and then a layer of compost. Put the plant in the container, making certain that the soil level is the same in the new container as it was in the old. Add compost around the sides of the pot, making sure that it is pressed firmly against all the roots. Firm the soil with your hands or a dibber, but don't ram the compost down too tightly. Rap the container down on a hard surface two or three times to shake out any air pockets. Water thoroughly and top up the level with more compost as it settles.

POTTING A PLANT

It can take a lot of compost to fill a large, deep container, and if you plan only to use bedding plants, for example, that root into just the top layer, you may be wasting money. Fill the bottom third to a half of the pot with broken up polystyrene plant trays, old bricks or rubble. Pour on coarse gravel or chippings

1 Add stones or broken crocks to the container to provide drainage.

2 Add compost to the bottom of the container so that the plant will sit a few centimetres below the rim of the pot.

Potting on

Young plants need to be transferred from small pots to larger pots, depending on their rate of growth. This should be done in stages. Always transfer a growing plant to a pot just larger than the one it is in at present, about 5cm (2in) diameter larger is ideal. This keeps the growth at a steady rate. If you potted on into a pot that was considerably larger, the roots would spread out too quickly, which upsets the growing balance of the plant.

Repotting

How often a plant should be repotted is a difficult question to answer. At one end of the scale, repotting may not be possible. Large raised beds, especially when they contain permanent trees or shrubs, cannot easily be emptied. In these cases remove as much of the top compost as possible without damaging the roots of the plant and then replace it with fresh compost and add fertilizer. Otherwise, in containers that can be moved, the compost should be emptied out and replaced every other year, and this should be done every year when the plant is growing vigorously.

until the surface is levelled and cover with fine plastic mesh to prevent soil washing down between the cracks. This method also ensures excellent drainage.

Alternatively, you could put a smaller pot inside the neck of the larger pot, hidden by the rim and if necessary supported on pebbles or gravel.

3 The best way to remove the plant from its original pot is to squeeze it and gently tip it out. Do not pull it out, as you may damage it.

4 Add compost around the plant, pushing it down firmly with your fingers. Water the container thoroughly.

HANDLING A DIFFICULT PLANT

Some container plants can prove tricky to handle – particularly if they are spiky or poisonous in any way. However, don't let this put you off cultivating or repotting any plant that takes your fancy, as with a little improvisation there is always a suitable method for handling even the most difficult of plants.

1 The following method is a good way to handle prickly plants, such as cacti, as well as plants with sap that can irritate skin. Cactus spines can cause discomfort for weeks and the easiest way to avoid this is by not touching the plant directly at all. Wrap a piece of folded newspaper or cloth round the plant and use it to cover the compost as the pot is inverted and knocked on a table edge to loosen the rootball.

2 Continue to leave the newspaper or cloth wrapped round the plant throughout the procedure as it is transferred to its new container, and then use it to hold the plant in place as new compost is added and firmed round the sides. Discard the cloth only once the whole operation is complete and the plant is safely in its new pot. Other awkward-to-handle plants can also be treated this way.

A clipped rosemary bush, trained into a ball. Training rosemary is complicated and has to be carried out carefully over a period of years.

Watering container plants

Watering is the most important part of container gardening and without water the plants will die. Indoors, use a watering can – regularly. Outdoors, if you can install an automatic watering system, this will solve all problems.

There is absolutely no point in attempting to grow plants in containers, outside, in the summer, unless you are able to water them every day. That is not to say that they have to be watered every day. If it rains all week you certainly won't, but if you go away on holiday for a fortnight and this coincides with a hot dry spell, don't be surprised if half the garden is dead when you return.

Plants grown in containers need far more moisture than plants grown in the garden. A large container 90cm (36in) in diameter may lose up to 5 litres (1.1 gallons) of water each day through the leaves of the plants (transpiration) and evaporation from the container itself, when it is hot and sunny.

Terracotta containers are more subject to evaporation than plastic ones, but you can overcome this if you line earthenware pots with plastic sheets when they are planted.

Technicalities

When you water both indoors and outdoors make sure that the container is watered thoroughly. Fill the container to the brim and let this drain down, then repeat. Do not over water. Check the condition of the compost rather than the plants. If they show signs of wilting they may be lacking in nutrients or may be waterlogged. If the compost feels dry to the touch more than 2.5cm (1in) below the surface, then water.

TIPS

1 Standing a pot on a container of gravel filled with water enables the plant to draw up the moisture it needs in a gradual way without the compost becoming waterlogged. This is the watering principle adopted in many greenhouses and it is ideal for indoor plants that need moisture and humidity.

2 If a plant appears totally dead and dried out, it is worth plunging the pot and plant in a bucket of water and leaving it there until the bubbles have stopped rising to the surface (right). There is a chance that it may well recover.

Watering systems

With a large container garden it is well worth installing an automatic watering system. These are computer-controlled and if you have one then all worries about watering vanish. There are three main systems: overhead sprinklers, trickle tubes, and capillary systems. All have their advantages and disadvantages. Overhead sprinklers are probably the cheapest to install but they use the most water. Trickle hoses are more expensive but more effective. They deliver water directly to the roots of the plants: there are small trickle systems for windowboxes and balconies.

Capillary systems, which supply water to the bottom of the plant, are used by nurseries and in greenhouses.

Tying a stake to a hosepipe will help you to reach high containers like hanging baskets.

Hoses, leaky hose systems and sprinklers can all be used to water containers.

Feeding container plants

Container-grown plants need additional feeding in order to thrive. Liquid fertilizer is the easiest to apply; check which nutrients are most needed.

All plants need nutrients to survive and grow. In the garden they will obtain most of their requirements from the soil, but because the area and soil volume in containers is limited and because they are watered more frequently, container-grown plants need regular feeding in order to perform well.

Basic chemistry

The three main nutrients required by plants are nitrogen (N), phosphorus (P) and potassium (K).

Nitrogen is essential for healthy leaf growth, phosphorus for the development of proper root systems and potassium promotes the production of flowers and fruit.

Plants also need a number of trace elements, the most important of which are manganese and magnesium. Nutrients are present in varying proportions in all fertilizers and foliar feeds and are marked on the label. A balanced fertilizer will contain them in equal proportions. A high potash (potassium) feed is excellent

APPLYING LIQUID FERTILIZERS

Liquid is usually easier and safer to apply than dry fertilizer, and the plant's response is often more rapid. The concentrated fertilizer is diluted in water. It is applied either to the soil or to the leaves, depending on the type. Mix the fertilizer thoroughly with the water before application, to reduce the chance of

damaging the plants. Do not apply when rain is forecast, or it may be washed through the soil away from the plant's roots. Foliar feeds are most effective during the summer and should be applied on the 'little and often' principle. Plants can be sprayed every fortnight with benefit.

1 Check the feed necessary for each plant and take care to apply the correct fertilizer at each stage of the plant's growth.

2 Growing plants need a nitrogen-based fertilizer but you should switch to a potash-(potassium) based fertilizer as the plants reach maturity.

for plants such as tomatoes and fruit bushes when the plants are mature and bearing fruit, while young plants, such as peppers, require high nitrogen feeds when they are growing to help them become established.

Apply fertilizers in liquid form during the growing season, use a liquid fertilizer or foliar feed. Slow-release granules, however, are invaluable. Add them to the soil at the start of the growing season and one application will serve many plants throughout the year.

Feeding requirements

Permanent plants need fertilizer incorporated in the compost when they are planted. If nutrients are not already present in the compost add bonemeal, Growmore, or fish, blood and bone.

Don't use fish, blood and bone or bonemeal if you live in an area where there are urban foxes for they will dig the plant up time and time again. After planting, all plants should be watered with a weak solution of fertilizer.

Herbs and vegetables

Most small herbs in pots will not require feeding other than an application of foliar food if the plants appear spindly or distressed. Vegetable crops grown in containers, on the other hand, need to be fed generously. They require nitrogen-based feeds when growth starts in spring followed by potassium-based fertilizer as the plants reach maturity.

Feeding indoor plants

Most indoor plants will require regular feeding. Begin feeding plants after six to eight weeks in a loamless compost and and 10–12 weeks in a loam-based one, and then feed regularly during the active growing and flowering season.

Liquid formulations come as a concentrate, as dry granules or powder to be diluted with, or dissolved in, water, and applied using a watering can, or in the case of a liquid foliar feed, a mist sprayer.

Feeding pins and spikes are pushed into the soil mix with the end of a pencil. However, take care not to place them too close to the roots of the plant, as localized burning can occur as a result of the high concentration of fertilizer.

Additional indoor plant care

During the warmer months, many indoor plants can be placed outside in containers, which will increase the variety of your summer displays. However. always check carefully for slugs, snails and other pests and diseases before bringing the plants back indoors, when the weather becomes cooler.

Once the plants have been brought back inside after their summer break outdoors, it is important to keep them clean and healthy, for example by regularly brushing the dust off leafy pot plants.

Mulching

Covering the surface of compost after planting conserves moisture, deters weeds and provides a decorative finish. This is known as mulching.

Mulching also helps to prevent erosion of the compost from the root system and sharp or gritty mulches may also deter slugs and snails. The only downside is that you have to scrape away some of the mulch if you want to check how dry the compost is beneath. Depending on the size of pot, use a 2–8cm (1–3in) layer of your chosen mulch, spreading it over the surface of moist compost. Avoid piling it up around the necks of plants.

Different types of mulch suit different planting and container styles. Here are some good combinations:

Gravel Available in different grades and colours so it should be easy to find one to match your container.

Pebbles Rounded pebbles and cobbles come in different shades and a variety of sizes to match the scale of the container and its planting.

Bark chips This is ideal for topdressing woodland style plantings, e.g. ferns and hostas in a wooden barrel.

Cocoa shells Similar to bark chips in appearance and use, they seem to be a good deterrent for slugs and snails.

Slate shards This material comes in several shades including purple, charcoal and green and provides an excellent mulch for contemporary style containers.

Gravel mulch
Covering the soil in your container with a mulch such as gravel will block out light and prevent weed seeds from germinating. It also helps to conserve moisture and can add a strong decorative element

1 Compost is not the most attractive material to look at so it can be useful to cover it with decorative mulches.

2 Very fine aquarium gravel is excellent for small areas and reflects light back up to the plant. It holds water so make sure you douse the area well enough for the water to soak right through to the compost.

3 Gravels vary enormously both in sizes and colours. Don't forget that they change colour when wet, so look at them both wet and dry before making a decision.

4 Traditional mulches are made up of chipped bark. It is great at suppressing weeds for a year or so but will rot down into the soil so will need to be replenished.

5 Peat moss is not peat; it is a form of moss that is cultivated for garden use. It gives a natural soft looking covering that will break down gradually adding nutrients to the soil.

6 Cocoa shell and bark mulches are much lighter in weight than most others, and the shells give off a wonderful scent of chocolate or rich woodland bark when first added to the pot.

Pruning, staking and supporting plants

Pruning is quite simple; the main thing is to prune at the correct time of the year and understand the requirements of each plant. Seek advice from a gardening neighbour or from a specialist book if in doubt.

Pruning in the container garden

Pruning causes more anxiety than any other gardening activity. However, once you understand the purpose and practice, pruning is perfectly simple and generally easy to effect.

Climbing plants

Roses: The best roses for a relatively restricted space are climbers with hybrid tea-shaped flowers or the climbing varieties of hybrid tea and floribunda roses. At planting trim any damaged roots, train in the shoots and tip back any damaged growth; cut out any weak side shoots. The following summer, tie in the side shoots as growth develops, train the shoots into a fan. Deadhead the rose after flowering. Early the following year cut back all the flowering laterals (side shoots) to 3–4 eyes or 15cm (6in) and tie in any shoots to form a framework. Repeat this on an annual basis, removing main branches after a year or two if they show signs of exhaustion to within 5cm (2in) of the ground. This stimulates new growth from the base.

Bougainvillea: Bougainvillea is a vigorous plant that will have to be cut back to keep it within bounds. After flowering, thin any old weak wood and cut out up to one-third of the shoots if necessary.

Passion flower: Prune after flowering. Cut back all the shoots that have flowered by one third. Cut out completely any shoots that appear weak or damaged.

Plumbago: A vigorous climber. Cut back hard in the spring by up to two-thirds of its height.

CORRECT PRUNING

Young plants can be pruned when first planted to a few strong shoots. Leave two buds on each pruned shoot and new growth will spring from them in the right direction the following year. Make sure that your secateurs are sharp and that the cuts are clean with no ragged edges as this can contribute to disease.

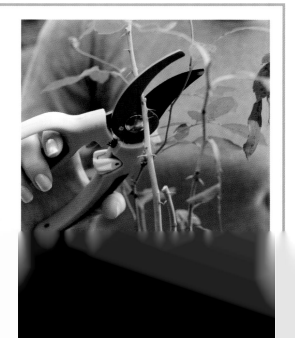

Climbing plants such as clematis, bougainvillea and passion flower will all benefit from regular pruning and general tidying up. Plants like these will rapidly outgrow even large containers unless they are properly tended.

Herbs and shrubs

Trim all shrubby herbs, such as thyme, sage and marjoram, to keep them neat in their containers in early spring; apart from this they do not need specific pruning.
Rosemary: Cut back any misplaced shoots in the spring but beware, rosemary will not regenerate if it is cut back into the hard wood.
Lavender: Prune lavender hard each mid-spring to stimulate new growth. Cut all flowering shoots right back to within 2.5cm (1in) of last year's wood.

Staking

Plants in containers do need staking to keep them in position. Push the stakes in down the sides of the containers and tie in each plant when it threatens to grow beyond its bounds. Large plants should be secured to walls, if possible, or tied in to a wire framework. Insert as large a stake as possible in the container when planting trees.

All trees and shrubs will need a supporting cane in place when they are first planted. All large trees require staking at planting.

Check that all plants are thoroughly secure. Small climbing plants can be trained up purpose-built trellises that can be inserted into the containers themselves or up trellises attached to walls.

Trellis supports

Trellis is available at all garden centres. Measure the amount you need and check that it is properly made. If you are erecting a trellis in a confined space, you may have to construct your own to ensure that it fits accurately and neatly. Secure it to the walls with Rawlplugs leaving a good 3.75cm (1¾in) gap for the air to circulate.

Supporting

Containers may blow over in high winds, especially if they are on an exposed roof garden and are top-heavy with trees or shrubs. It is most important to ensure that all containers are supported securely and it may be necessary to secure them with guy ropes or wire fastened to ring bolts on the roof or walls of the garden.

Trimming and shaping

Many trees and shrubs grown in containers will benefit from regular trimming and shaping in order to maintain their form and keep them looking their best. Attractive topiary effects can easily be achieved with a number of plants, particulary box, which can be clipped and lightly pruned into any number of different shapes. Regular trimming is also good for the health of many plants.

The decorative effect of plants can be enhanced by training or clipping to a more formal shape. Use potted topiary to add emphasis to the garden's design, for example, placing a matching pair of standards to strengthen a doorway or a row of clipped globes to create a pleasing rhythm along the edge of a path.

Simple topiary

Many small-leaved evergreens can be clipped into simple geometric forms, such as balls, domes and cones. You only need a few simple tools – secateurs, small or ladies' hand shears or one-handed 'sheep' shears. Box (*Buxus sempervirens*), is a classic topiary plant that is sufficiently fine-textured and dense to allow for more complex forms including spirals. You could also consider the following plants:

Euonymus fortunei 'Emerald Gaiety' and 'Emerald 'n' Gold'
Hebe, e.g. *H. toparia; H. rakaiensis*
Ilex aquifolium
Ilex crenata
Laurus nobilis
Ligustrum delavayanum
Myrtus communis
Osmanthus heterophylla
Osmanthus x *burkwoodii*
Pittosporum tenuifolium
Pittosporum tobira
Santolina chamaecyparissus
Viburnum tinus

Use secateurs to shape larger-leaved plants such as bay, holly and viburnum. To clip balls or domes, stand above the plant and turn the shears upside down so that the shape of the blade follows the curve. Keep walking round and standing back to view. Trim flowering and berrying shrubs after the display and avoid shaping evergreens between the end of summer and mid- to late spring, as otherwise the soft re-growth might not withstand frosts.

Since bay leaves are quite big and their appearance would be spoiled if leaves were damaged, it is best to prune them with secateurs rather than clipping them with shears.

SHAPING A BOX PLANT

Box is a very popular and easily managed traditional topiary subject. Use *Buxus sempervirens* and not the miniature cultivar 'Suffruticosa'. To shape existing box bushes growing in the garden or fair-sized bushy plants from garden centres, the best technique is to choose a plant that already suggests a simple shape, such as a bun or a sphere, and simply exaggerate that by light clipping. The easiest way to create more complicated shapes is to start with a very small plant.

1 -Start with a strong, rooted box cutting. Neatly nip off the growing tips of the shoots using your thumb and forefinger. Repeat as the shoots grow.

2 -Use secateurs to nip back the tips of the next crop of sideshoots, so that each time the new growth reaches 5cm (2in) long it is shortened.

3 -As the first pot becomes filled with roots, move the plant into a larger pot. Continue clipping regularly with small shears.

4 -When it reaches the required size, clip back to the previous outline each time. By then, clipping three or four times a year should be sufficient.

General care and maintenance

Looking after your outdoor garden containers is very important. They need to be kept clean and well drained. Support them on chocks to allow the air to circulate underneath and this will prolong their life.

All containers must be suitable for their purpose. They must fit the plant and they must contain sufficient compost in order for that plant to flourish. They must be strong enough to withstand the elements. They must also have adequate drainage to allow surplus water to drain away when the plants are watered.

Drainage

Almost all garden containers that you can purchase will have proper drainage holes already in place, but if they don't you will have to make holes in the bottom. The same goes if you have made the containers yourself. Make sure that there are enough drainage holes and if you are lining the container with polythene see that there are holes in the polythene that align with the holes in the bottom of the container.

The correct hardcore

Prepared containers must include sufficient hardcore, crocks, broken pottery or small stones in the bottom to keep the compost aerated and ensure that it does not run out of the drainage holes when the container is watered.

Make sure that any hardcore material used in the bottom of a pot of ericaceous compost does not contain any lime. For example, limestone chippings and old mortar are obvious sources of lime and should be avoided.

Cleaning

Containers should be cleaned after use to prevent the spread of disease. Scrub them thoroughly to remove all dirt and if necessary soak them overnight in soapy water. Ensure that they are completely dry before filling and re-using.

Cleaning a used pot

1 Remove any old growing medium and plant debris by scrubbing the pot, inside and out, with a wire brush or stiff household brush.

2 Wash the container thoroughly with detergent and warm water, then rinse well with clean water before refilling with fresh growing medium.

Wooden containers

These need to be treated with a preservative recommended for horticultural use before they are first planted. Make sure that you use one that is safe with plants and follow the instructions on the label. Preservatives such as creosote should be avoided at all costs, as they will kill any plants.

You can also extend the life of a wooden container by lining it with plastic. Make holes in the bottom of the plastic for drainage and then fix it to the sides of the container with a staple gun.

It is also a good idea to line the sides of any copper, iron or lead containers that you are using in order to prevent the metallic elements of the container leaching into the compost, which might affect the plants.

Allow air to circulate

Raise all containers off the ground slightly, in order to promote drainage and allow air to circulate, by putting them on wooden chocks or special clay feet. This is a particularly important consideration for wooden containers, because if they are allowed to sit permanently in damp, they will gradually rot.

Moving containers

Large containers full of plants can be heavy and difficult to move. There are a number of ways to do this. You can try and manoeuvre the container on to a piece of sacking and then pull the sacking to where you want it to be. You can put it on a board and then put small rollers under the board in the same way as boats used to be launched, or you can make a rope cradle round the container, attach the ends to a strong pole and lift it with the help of a couple of strong people. In all these cases you may want to wrap up the plants to protect them while they are being moved.

In order for your plants to look their best, it is important to keep their containers in tip-top condition. These terracotta pots could do with a good clean in order to make the most of the mixed herbs that they contain. Of course, if you choose instead to go for a weathered, aged look to your pots and containers, then don't clean them at all! Indeed, you can enhance the look by applying yogurt and allowing algae to grow on the terracotta or other material (see page 10).

Pests and diseases

These are the major pests, diseases and other problems that affect flowering container plants. However, do not be alarmed, as although there are numerous things to be concerned about, your plants are unlikely to be troubled by all of these. For proven environmental reasons, there is a strong emphasis in these pages on non-chemical methods of control of the pests and diseases discussed.

Aphids

These are among the most troublesome of insect pests, particularly greenfly and blackfly, and they attack a wide range of flowers. Wash off aphids with plain or soapy water, or spray with insecticidal soap if necessary (neither harms beneficial insects).

Black root rot

A disease affecting many flowers. The roots become black, but above-ground symptoms are yellowing and wilting leaves. Scrap sickly looking plants and plant something different in the affected site.

Bulb aphids

Certain aphids winter on bulbs and corms in store. Look out for them on crocuses, gladioli, lilies and tulips especially, and simply rub them off.

Bulb rot

Bulbs of various kinds, including daffodils, lilies and tulips, are prone to rotting in store, caused by various diseases. Check for soft spots, particularly at the base of the bulbs (basal rot). Remove and discard rotting bulbs.

Caterpillars

The caterpillars of various moths and butterflies eat holes in the leaves of numerous perennials and annuals. They are generally green, brown or grey and are usually hairy. Caterpillars are easily picked off and destroyed, or plants can be sprayed with an insecticide if necessary.

Corm rot

Corms such as crocuses and gladioli are prone to several kinds of rot while in store, so check regularly and remove and discard any that show signs of rot.

Cutworms

These caterpillars, the larvae of several different moths and greenish brown or greyish brown in colour, live in the soil and feed on roots and stem bases of plants, causing young plants to wilt and die. Remove any found during soil cultivations.

Damping off

This disease affects seedlings indoors, causing them to suddenly collapse and die. Damping off can spread rapidly and should be prevented by using sterilized compost and clean containers.

Earwigs

These night-feeding insects, easily recognized by their rear pincers, eat holes in flowers, buds and leaves. Remove and destroy any pests. Spray plants with an insecticide if necessary.

Foot rot

This disease causes the bases of stems to turn black and rot. Pull up and discard any plants that show signs of infection.

Grey mould

This major fungal disease, also known as botrytis, can infect all top growth of plants – flowers, buds, leaves and stems – resulting in rotting. Cut off any affected parts of plants, back to healthy tissue.

Leaf spot

Many diseases show up as brown or black spots on the leaves of numerous ornamental plants. The spots vary in size and some are in the form of rings. The best control method is to pick off any leaves showing spots. Spray affected plants with fungicide if necessary.

Mildew

The most common is powdery mildew, appearing as white powdery patches on the leaves of many plants. Remove affected leaves. Spray plants with fungicide if necessary.

Petal blight

This disease attacks chrysanthemums, and sometimes other related plants, and anemones, showing as watery lesions or brown spots on the petals. Remove affected flowers. Spray plants with fungicide if necessary.

Red spider mite

There are several kinds of these microscopic spider-like creatures that feed by sucking the sap from the leaves of many plants, particularly under glass. This results in fine pale yellow mottling on the upper leaf surfaces. Spraying plants regularly with plain water will deter the mites. Or spray plants with insecticidal soap.

Rhizome rot

This bacterial disease causes the leaves of rhizomatous irises to turn yellow and wither. Dig up and discard badly affected plants. Avoid damaging surrounding plants as you do this.

Rust

This fungal disease shows as rust-coloured, orange, yellow or dark brown raised spots on the leaves and stems. Affected leaves should be removed. Spray with a fungicide if necessary.

Slugs and snails

Slugs and snails eat the leaves of a wide range of plants and also damage soft young stems and even flowers. Control by placing slug pellets around plants. Alternatively, remove them by hand.

Stem rot

Numerous diseases, but particularly sclerotinia, cause the stems of various perennials and annuals to rot. As there is no cure, plants that are badly affected should be removed and discarded.

Tuber rot

A fungal disease may attack dahlias in store, causing the tubers to rot. Check stored tubers regularly and, if rotting is noticed, cut it away to healthy tissue.

Viruses

Viruses are types of diseases that infect a wide range of plants. The most common symptoms are stunted and distorted plants. There is no cure: pull up and burn affected plants.

Weevils

These beetles are easily recognized by their elongated 'snout'. Their larvae are the main problem. Their feeding causes wilting, and invariably death in severe attacks. Use biological control with a pathogenic nematode in late summer.

Wilting leaves

Apart from wilting caused by various pests and diseases, the most common cause is drought. Young plants may never recover, even if watering is carried out. Make sure the soil never dries out, ideally by mulching permanent plants and by watering as necessary.

Woodlice

These pests feed at night and hide in dark places during the day. Physical control is not practical, except to ensure that any plant debris is not left lying around, which will encourage their appearance.

Indoor Plants

Achimenes erecta
Cupid's bower

Also known as Nut orchid and Magic flower, Cupid's bower can produce a spectacular display of flowers and foliage. It grows from small rhizomes, each of which sends up one reddish-green stem, carrying pairs of heart-shaped, dark green, and hairy leaves. The bright red flowers last for only a few days but are produced over a period lasting from June to October. This variety grows well in a hanging basket in a warm, well-lit place, or it can be made to bush by tying the stems to short canes and pinching the shoots regularly.

Care
Keep the soil moist throughout spring to autumn but do not water in the winter. Water with standard liquid fertilizer every two weeks during spring to autumn.

New plants
Take tip cuttings or pieces of rhizome around 7.5cm (3in) in length in spring to summer and plant in a sterile medium in individual pots.

H 45cm (18in)

15–25°C
(60–80°F)

Partial
shade

Argyranthemum
Madeira series Marguerite

This attractive, compact plant with its wide, daisy-like flowers and divided, matt green foliage, is a wonderfully colourful addition to any indoor display. Unlike its larger predecessors, which originated as garden plants, the new Argyranthemum Madeira series has been developed with indoor and greenhouse use in mind. There are 11 varieties in the series, including 'Santana' (rose-red with a yellow centre), 'Machio' (double, pink), and 'Sao Martinho' (anemone-form, creamy white). They will flower profusely throughout the summer and thrive in a cooler situation, as long as they have good light. They actually produce better flower colours in slightly lower temperatures.

Care
Keep the compost moist at all times. Feed with standard liquid tomato fertilizer at half strength every two weeks from spring to late summer. Pinch out growing tips when the plant is young to produce a bushier plant.

New plants
Best treated as an annual and replaced each year.

Begonia x hiemalis
Winter-flowering begonia

Although the common name of this plant suggests that it flowers only in the winter, improvements in breeding mean that it is now available in flower all year round. It is fibrous-rooted with single or double flowers. It ranges in colour from white to pink, yellow-orange or red. The leaves are usually a glossy pale green, but plants with darker-coloured flowers also tend to have darker, more bronzy foliage.

Care
Keep the compost moist, but not wet – overwatering can cause rotting. Feed with standard liquid fertilizer every two weeks during spring to summer. Keep out of direct sunlight, which can cause scorching on the leaves.

New plants
Take tip cuttings 7–10cm (3–4in) long from non-flowering shoots, and root in seed and cutting compost.

Other varieties
Begonia bowerae is a bushy, stemless plant grown for its attractive foliage rather than its flowers, which are small and pale pink. High humidity is important, so stand the pot on a tray of moist pebbles and mist regularly. Good hygiene is critical where humidity is high, because grey mould thrives in such conditions.

H & S
30–35cm
(12–14in)

15–25°C
(60–80°F)

Partial shade

H 45cm (18in)
S 30cm (12in)

15–25°C
(60–80°F)

Partial shade

Bougainvillea glabra
Paper flower

Bougainvilleas are woody, spiny plants that originate in the subtropical areas of South America and need high levels of both warmth and light in order to flourish. They are also vigorous growers, although regular pruning and training will keep them smaller and more bushy. Given good conditions, they will produce their vividly coloured bracts – which surround the insignificant cream flowers – in clusters of 10–20 throughout the spring and summer. The bracts are in shades of white, pink, red or purple. Other varieties include *B. glabra* 'Variegata', which has grey-green leaves splashed with cream; *B. glabra* 'Magnifica', with vivid purple bracts; and *B. glabra* 'Sanderiana', which has long-lasting magenta bracts.

Care
Keep compost thoroughly moist from spring to autumn but apply only enough water to prevent drying out in winter. Feed with standard liquid fertilizer every two weeks from spring to summer. Leaf loss in winter is normal, but at any other time it indicates that all is not well in terms of growing conditions. To reduce excessive growth, cut long shoots back to two or three buds in early spring and reduce the rest of the growth by one third.

New plants
Take tip cuttings 15cm (6in) long in spring, transplant and place in a heated propagator. Rooting should take six to eight weeks.

Campanula isophylla
Star of Bethlehem

Also known as Falling stars and Italian bellflower, this is a pretty, trailing form of campanula that looks equally good tumbling from a pot or hanging basket. The star-shaped flowers are produced throughout summer and autumn. They are usually violet-blue, although *Campanula isophylla* 'Alba', a white form, is also available. There is also a double form, *C. isophylla* 'Flore Pleno'. The stems and leaves of campanula are bright green and slightly brittle. If they are broken, they exude a distinctive smell and a milky-white sap.

Care
Keep the compost thoroughly moist during spring to autumn but slightly drier in winter. Feed with standard liquid fertilizer every two weeks from late spring to autumn. Removing flowers as they fade helps to prolong the flowering period. Once flowering has finished in autumn, cut the stems back hard, close to the base.

New plants
Take tip cuttings 5cm (2in) long in spring and root in seed and cutting compost.

H To 3m (10ft)

15–17°C (60–62°F)

Direct sunlight

H 30cm (12in)
S 30cm (12in)

15–17°C (60–62°F)

Partial shade

Cattleya

Orchid

These are a group of evergreen epiphytic orchids that produce pseudobulbs on short rhizomes. The leaves are leathery, semi-rigid, and mid- to dark green, produced singly or in pairs. The flowers are large and showy, with three-lobed or entire central 'lips'. They are borne singly or in clusters at the ends of the shoots, and there are hundreds of hybrids to choose from, in colours ranging from white through yellow, gold, orange, pink, mauve and purple to shades of green. There is often a contrasting flush of colour on the lips.

Care

Grow in fine-grade epiphytic orchid compost in a container or slatted basket. From spring to autumn, water and mist daily. In winter, water sparingly. Feed with standard liquid fertilizer once a week.

New plants

Divide the mature plant when it fills the pot and transplant the separate parts.

Clivia miniata

Bush lily

Dark green leaves that grow to a length of 60cm (24in) make this an impressive indoor plant even when it is not in flower. But keep in mind that it does need space to develop. It should not be moved while the flowers are maturing or when they open. The 45cm (18in) flower stalk appears in spring, carrying up to 15 broadly funnel-shaped flowers, each bright scarlet with a yellow throat and up to 7.5cm (3in) long.

Care

In order to flower, it is important that this plant has a winter rest period of six to eight weeks at 5–10°C (40–50°F). Not observing the winter rest results in short, premature flowers or a shortened flower life. Keep moist during spring to autumn. In winter, keep almost dry until the flower stalk appears, then increase watering. Feed with standard liquid fertilizer every two weeks from when the flower stalk is 10–15cm (4–6in) high until autumn. Remove any fruits, which will sap so much of the plant's energy that they will reduce flowering the following year.

New plants

Divide the mature plant or detach offsets immediately after flowering, taking care not to damage fleshy roots. Root in seed and cutting compost in individual pots.

H 30cm (12in)
S 30cm (12in)

15–17°C
(60–62°F)

Partial
shade

H 45cm (18in)
S 90cm (36in)

15–17°C
(60–62°F)

Partial
shade

Cyclamen persicum
Cyclamen

Known as the 'florist's cyclamen', these plants come in a variety of shapes and sizes. The nodding flowers can be ruffled, twisted, speckled and sometimes scented, in shades of pure white to purple through a range of reds and pinks. The fleshy, dark green leaves can be large or tiny and usually have silver patterns. Often sold at Christmas, the cyclamen should last several weeks in flower – but do not buy from an outdoor vendor, because if the plant is chilled, the flowering period will be shortened.

Care
Keep the compost moist by watering from below because the tuber is only half-buried in the soil mix, and watering from above may cause it to rot. Feed with standard liquid fertilizer every two weeks. Hygiene is critical to prevent grey mould, so as the flowers fade or the leaves die, remove immediately by twisting off as close as possible to the base.

New plants
Small plants can be raised from seed, but these cyclamen are usually bought as mature flowering plants.

H 20cm (8in)
S 15cm (6in)

12–18°C
(55–65°F)

Partial shade

Gardenia jasminoides
Gardenia

This is a bushy, evergreen, acid-loving shrub, grown for its waxy flowers, which are up to 7.5cm (3in) across, white and intensely fragrant. They are usually double – many-petalled – but also occur as two layers of petals. The lance-shaped, dark green leaves are 5–10cm (2–4in) long, glossy and leathery. *Gardenia jasminoides* 'Radicans Variegata' is a miniature form that grows into a mound shape and has small white flowers and leaves that are glossy, tinted grey, and edged in white. *G. jasminoides* 'Veitchiana' is a more upright and compact form, with small, pure white, fully double and very fragrant flowers and small, bright green leaves.

Care
While flower buds are forming, a constant, draught-free 17°C (62–63°F) is needed to prevent bud loss. Otherwise, normal room temperature is fine. Keep the compost moist during spring to autumn, using soft water or rainwater. High humidity is essential while the flower buds are forming, so stand the pot on a tray of moist pebbles, and mist frequently. In winter, apply only sufficient water to prevent the compost drying out. Feed with acid fertiliser every 2 weeks from spring to autumn. Any pruning should be done immediately after flowering; cut to an outward-facing bud.

H 45cm (18in)
S 30cm (12in)

16–18°C
(62–64°F)

Partial shade

Impatiens New Guinea hybrids

Bizzy Lizzy

Larger than the traditional impatiens and almost shrubby in habit, the dramatic New Guinea hybrids bear the same characteristics: constant flowering from a young age, brittle succulent-looking stems and lush, fleshy foliage. They are bolder and more colourful, with leaves that may be bright green, green splashed with yellow, or a bronze-red colour. The flowers are larger, with a prominent spur, generally single, and come in many shades of red, pink, mauve and white.

Care
Keep the compost moist from spring to autumn. In winter, apply only sufficient water to prevent it from drying out. Feed with a standard liquid fertilizer every two weeks during spring to autumn. Too warm a location will cause rapid wilting, so stand pots on a tray of moist pebbles to increase humidity.

New plants
Take 10cm (4in) tip cuttings in spring or summer and root in water or potting compost.

H 45cm (18in)
S 60cm (24in)

16–18°C
(62–64°F)

Direct
sunlight

Narcissus spp.

Narcissus, Daffodil

The genus Narcissus is enormous and highly varied in both size and flower form, ranging from tiny 10cm (4in) dwarf types to traditional, tall garden varieties of 60cm (24in) high. Many can be brought into flower with great success indoors, especially in a conservatory or greenhouse where they can enjoy cool, well-lit conditions, and many are also very good for growing in outdoor containers. The flowers come in shades of yellow, white, orange, cream and, more recently, pink, and can be single or clustered, with single or double petals and varying lengths and shapes of trumpet. Recommended varieties as houseplants are *Narcissus* 'Tete-a-Tete', 15–30cm (6–12in) high with yellow, multi-headed flowers; *N.* 'Sundial', 15–30 cm (6–12in) high with wide, yellow flowers; *N.* 'Paperwhite' which is 30–45cm (12–18in) high and has white, highly scented flowers; and *N.* 'Bridal Crown', 30–45cm (12–18in) high with cream double flowers.

Care
Keep the compost moist at all times. Apply liquid fertilizer at half strength once a week from flower opening until the leaves turn yellow.

New plants
Remove offsets as the leaves die down in late spring or in early autumn as you plant the bulbs.

H 10–60cm
(4–24in)

16–18°C
(62–64°F)

Direct
sunlight

Passiflora 'Amethyst'
Passion flower

This is a beautiful, vigorous climbing plant with smooth, slender stems and deeply three-lobed leaves of a rich mid-green. In late summer and autumn, it produces wide-open amethyst purple flowers up to 10cm (4in) across, with green anthers and sepals that reflex as the flower matures. The flowers are followed by egg-shaped orange fruits up to 6cm (2½in) long. This plant is hardy in many areas but makes a spectacular addition to the conservatory, cool greenhouse or well-lit porch.

Care
Water freely from spring until autumn; then apply only enough water to prevent the compost drying out. Water with standard liquid fertilizer once a month during spring and early summer.

New plants
Take semi-ripe cuttings in summer, and root in seed and cutting compost.

Other varieties
P. caerulea is a vigorous plant with deep green, angular stems, which climbs by using twisting tendrils. It flowers while still young, producing five white sepals and five white petals of equal length, surrounding a circle of filaments shaded blue-purple, with a white band in the middle.

H To 4m (13ft)

16–18°C (62–64°F)

Direct sunlight

Pelargonium x *domesticum*
Geranium

This is a large group of hybrids of complicated origins, with thick, branching stems and hairy, toothed leaves up to 10cm (4in) across. The flowers are large and showy, borne in upright clusters, in single or combined shades of white, pink, salmon, orange, red or purple. They are usually single, and the upper petals are often blotched with a darker colour. These plants can also be grown outdoors during the summer months. *Pelargonium* 'Carisbrooke' has large pink flowers marked with wine red; *P.* 'Grand Slam' has rose-red flowers with darker markings; *P.* 'Pompeii' is a compact plant, which has nearly black petals with narrow pink-white edges.

Care
Water moderately and allow to dry slightly between watering. Feed with standard liquid fertilizer at half strength every two weeks from spring to late summer.

New plants
Take tip or stem cuttings in spring or early summer, and remove small stipules and leaves from the lower third of the stem. Allow to wilt for 30 minutes before inserting into potting compost. Do not use rooting hormone on cuttings, because they contain naturally high levels of hormone and adding extra will make the stem rot.

H To 45cm (18in)

16–18°C
(62–64°F)

Partial
shade

Plumbago auriculata
Cape leadwort

This is an evergreen shrub, with long, arching stems that need to be tied to supports to prevent them from straggling. Pretty sky-blue flowers are borne in clusters of up to 20 throughout spring, summer and autumn amid long oval, mid-green leaves. The individual flowers are tubular, flaring out into five petals, each of which is marked with a darker blue central stripe. *Plumbago auriculata* 'Alba' is a form with pure white flowers.

Care
Keep thoroughly moist in spring to autumn. In winter, apply only sufficient water to prevent the compost drying out.

Fertilize with a high-potash fertilizer, such as tomato fertilizer, every two weeks from spring to summer. Remove flowers as they fade to promote the production of more buds. Flowers are produced on the current season's growth, so any pruning should be done in early spring to give the maximum flowering time. When pruning, reduce growth by up to two-thirds.

New plants
Take 7.5–10cm (3–4in) cuttings in spring or summer. Alternatively air layer the stem, or sow seed.

H To 3m (10ft)

16–18°C
(62–64°F)

Direct
sunlight

Primula obconica
German primrose, Poison primrose

This is a pretty plant for indoors; it produces masses of large, fragrant blooms during the early months of the year in shades of white, pink, salmon, lilac, magenta or red, each with a distinctive apple-green eye. They can be grouped together for instant effect or used to add short-term colour to a more permanent foliage arrangement. The flowers are borne in clusters on 30cm (12in) stalks emerging from leaves that are roughly circular in shape, coarse in texture, and covered with fine hairs. The fine hairs that cover the leaves may cause skin irritation.

Care
Keep the compost thoroughly moist. Feed with standard liquid fertilizer every two weeks. Picking off the flowers as they fade will prolong the flowering period. *Primula obconica* is usually treated as an annual and discarded after flowering, but it can be brought back for a second year by keeping it cool and barely moist after flowering until autumn, when it can be repotted and the watering increased.

New plants
Sow seed in spring, but it is not easy to grow.

H To 30cm (12in)

10–12°C
(50–55°F)

Partial shade

Rhododendron simsii

Indian azalea

This is the florist's azalea, which is found in large quantities and a wide range of colours throughout winter and spring each year. It gives a spectacular display, with a succession of flowers over a period of about six weeks in shades of white, pink, red, purple or a combination. Each individual bloom lasts several days. Buy a plant with only a few open blooms – to ascertain the colour – and plenty of buds, to ensure the best display.

Care

This plant needs to be kept wet, not just moist, in order to thrive. They are acid-loving plants and may begin to suffer if they are watered with hard tap water. Using rainwater will help if the leaves begin to turn yellow (chlorosis). Repot into an ericaceous soil mix once flowering is over. Feed with standard liquid fertilizer every two weeks in spring to summer, then once a month in autumn. Remove only the petals of the faded flowers when deadheading. The new shoots that follow the flowers arise from the same point on the stem, so cutting off the whole flower head will remove the shoot buds, too.

New plants

Take 5cm (2in) tip cuttings in late spring from the new growth. Use rooting hormone and pot in ericaceous compost.

H 30–45cm
(12–18in)

7–15°C
(45–60°F)

Partial
shade

Rosa chinensis
Fairy rose

There is a tendency to view roses as outdoor plants, but the miniature varieties make excellent indoor flowering specimens, giving colour and fragrance throughout the summer. The flowers can be single, semi-double, or fully double, with colours that include red, pink, yellow, white and a range of shades in between. After flowering, they can be planted in the garden or, with a little attention, kept for future use indoors.

Care
Keep the compost moist during spring to autumn. High humidity is important, so stand the pot on a tray of moist pebbles. In winter, apply only sufficient water to prevent it drying out. Feed with standard liquid fertilizer every two weeks in spring to summer. If the plant is to be kept indoors, it will need a winter rest period of eight weeks at 7°C (45°F) or lower. To bring the plant back into flower indoors a second year, repot in autumn and set the plant outside. Bring indoors in January, acclimatizing gradually if possible, rather than putting it straight into a warm room. Prune to outward-facing buds to shorten each stem by half, increase watering and feeding, and the plant could be in flower by early spring.

New plants
Take 5cm (2in) tip cuttings in spring, use a rooting hormone, and root in seed and cutting compost.

| H To 30cm (12in) |
| 15–17°C (60–62°F) |
| Direct sunlight |

Thunbergia alata
Black-eyed Susan

This is a reliable, quick-growing, twining plant, normally grown as an annual, which gives a colourful display of flowers throughout the summer and will easily cover a screen or trellis. It grows well indoors as well as outdoors in the summer months. The toothed leaves are triangular, surrounding flowers that are trumpet-shaped and up to 5cm (2in) across in shades of orange, yellow or white, each with a chocolate-brown eye. Several plants can be grown together in a container on a tepee of canes to give an impressive splash of colour. Single plants can be grown up strings in a window or allowed to trail gracefully from a hanging basket.

Care
Keep the compost thoroughly moist. Feed with standard liquid fertilizer every two weeks. Pinch out the flowers as they fade to ensure more are produced.

New plants
Sow seed in seed and cutting compost in spring.

| H To 2.1m (7ft) |
| 15–17°C (60–62°F) |
| Direct sunlight |

Adiantum raddianum

Maidenhair fern

This is the most popular fern for growing indoors. It gets its common name because the shiny dark leaf stalks resemble human hair. The dark green, triangular fronds are semi-erect at first, drooping gracefully as they age, and can be up to 20cm (8in) long by 15cm (6in) wide. This is a pretty, delicate plant in its own right but complements, fills and softens when added to other arrangements. To grow well, it needs moist air, warmth and shade and will prefer to live in a greenhouse or bathroom rather than the living room or hallway.

Care
Keep the compost moist, but do not allow it to become waterlogged. Ferns cannot thrive if they are neglected.

They need both moist air and compost: dry air, gas fumes and cold draughts will harm them, as will allowing the compost to dry out and then soaking it. Remove older fronds as their appearance deteriorates – a few at a time from right at their base in spring each year to allow space for new shoots to develop. This fern also benefits from monthly feeding throughout the growing season.

New plants
Divide older clumps in spring or break off new clumps from the rhizome with one or two fronts attached. Pot up individually.

H 45cm (18in)
S 60cm (24in)

15–20°C
(60–70°F)

Partial shade

Allamanda carthartica
Golden trumpet

This vigorous climbing plant is probably best suited to a warm greenhouse, where it can grow to its full height or be trained against a wall, although it can also easily be trained to a support or frame. The leaves are a glossy dark green, oval in shape, and 10–15cm (4–6in) long. The flowers are produced throughout the summer and are a spectacular golden yellow, marked white in the throat. Other varieties include *A. carthartica* 'Grandiflora', which has more compact, large flowers, *A. carthartica* 'Hendersonii', which has buds tinged bronze and orange-yellow flowers; and *A. carthartica* 'Nobilis', which has very large bright gold flowers and large, glossy leaves.

Care
Keep the compost moist during spring to autumn but allow it to dry slightly in winter. Feed with standard liquid fertilizer every two weeks in spring to summer. This is quite a strong-growing plant, so it can be cut down by two-thirds in winter.

New plants
Take tip cuttings 7.5–10cm (3–4in) long in spring, pot in seed and cutting compost and cover with a plastic bag or place in a propagator. Keep the cuttings at 70°F (21°C), in bright light.

H To 6m (20ft)

16–18°C
(62–64°F)

Direct
sunlight

Asparagus densiflorus 'Sprengeri'

Emerald fern

This is a delicate, fern-like plant, with woody stems that can be erect or trailing. The feathery emerald-green foliage is prized by flower arrangers, but it is also useful among a group of other indoor plants to soften the display and add contrast. The flowers are small and insignificant but are sometimes followed by bright red fruits. Although the term 'fern' appears in the name, these are not true ferns and are actually in the lily family.

Caring for plants

Keep the compost thoroughly moist during spring to autumn, but during the winter, give only sufficient water to prevent drying out. Feed with standard liquid fertilizer every two weeks during spring to autumn. Keep out of direct sun, which will scorch the foliage.

Making new plants

Divide larger plants in spring and repot the individual clumps.

Citrus limon

Lemon

Lemons ultimately grow into small trees, but while they are young, they make attractive indoor plants, producing flowers and fruit intermittently all year when conditions are right. They have glossy, deep green, oval-shaped foliage and spiny stems. The flowers are white tinged with purple and fragrant, with five blunt petals and large stamens. Each fruit ripens slowly from green to yellow, so that there will be fruit of various sizes and colour shades on the plant at the same time. Their palatability depends on the variety. To grow edible fruit of a good size, choose a named variety.

Care

Keep moist during spring to autumn. In winter, apply only sufficient water to prevent the compost from drying out. To increase the humidity, stand the pot on a tray of moist pebbles. Pinching out the growing tips at regular intervals will produce bushy growth. Fertilize with citrus fertilizer every two weeks from spring to autumn.

New plants

Take tip cuttings 10 cm (4 in) long in spring to summer, preferably semi-ripe with a heel, and dip in hormone rooting powder before rooting in seed and cutting compost. Also sow seed from the fruits, although these will take longer to grow to flowering size.

H To 45cm (18in)

15–20°C (60–70°F)

Partial shade

H To 2.1m (7ft)

15–17°C (60–62°F)

Direct sunlight

Cyperus involucratus
Umbrella grass

This is a clump-forming perennial with short basal leaves. It forms small, leafy bracts on the ends of tall, hollow green stems up to 75cm (30in) long. In summer, it produces yellow flowers that turn brown after releasing their pollen, surrounded by up to 30 long bracts on top of long, three-sided stems. The bracts are arranged spirally, like the spokes of an umbrella. It is an unusual foliage plant, ideal for adding height to a group display.

Care
Keep thoroughly moist at all times. This plant needs high humidity, so stand the container on a saucer of pebbles and keep the water level in the saucer high so it can evaporate around the leaves. Feed with standard liquid fertilizer once a month during spring and early summer.

New plants
Divide mature plants in spring, and plant up pieces in potting compost in individual pots.

Cyperus papyrus
Papyrus, Egyptian paper reed

Used for papermaking since ancient times, this is a large, clump-forming plant that needs plenty of space to grow to full size. It also needs a very moist environment and will thrive in boggy conditions, although it should not be completely submerged. The dark green 'leaves' are actually bracts, borne at the top of tall, triangular stems, and above these are the flowers, which are carried in grasslike clusters.

Care
Overwatering this plant is almost impossible, and its great demand for both water and humidity can be taken care of by standing the pot in a tray or saucer full of water. The plant can then take up as much water as it needs and the remains will increase the humidity. Feed with standard liquid fertilizer once a month during spring to autumn. Dry air or drying out of the rootball will result in brown tips on the bracts.

New plants
Divide mature plants in spring, and keep the potting compost moist.

H 75cm (30in)
S 60cm (24in)

15–17°C (60–62°F)

Partial shade

H To 3m (10ft)

15–17°C (60–62°F)

Direct sunlight

Exacum affine

Persian violet, German violet

This is a short-lived perennial plant, generally treated as an annual and discarded after flowering. It has glossy green leaves and an abundance of fragrant sky-blue to pale violet or rich purple flowers with prominent golden stamens. If the plant is in bud when bought, it will flower throughout summer and autumn.

Care

Keep the compost thoroughly moist. Exacum likes high humidity, so stand the pot on a tray of moist pebbles. Feed with standard liquid fertilizer every two weeks while the plant is in flower. Pick off fading flowers to extend the flowering period.

New plants

Sow seed in late summer for the following year or in spring for a slightly later flowering in the same year – at a temperature of 25°C (80°F).

H 30cm (12in)
S 60cm (24in)

15–17°C
(60–62°F)

Partial shade

Pentas lanceolata

Egyptian star cluster

This is an attractive and unusual soft-wooded shrub with 10cm (4in) long, hairy, lance-shaped leaves. The flowers are borne in 10cm (4in) clusters. Each individual, tubular bloom opens out in a 5-pointed star shape, measuring 12mm (½in) across, usually in autumn and winter but also at other times. The flowers can be shades of magenta, red, mauve, pink or white, according to the variety.

Care

Keep moist throughout the year except for a six to eight week period immediately after flowering, when only sufficient water should be applied to prevent the compost drying out. Feed with standard liquid fertilizer once a month all year except during the rest period. Pinching out the shoot tips regularly will produce a bushy plant.

New plants

Take 7.5–10cm (3–4in) tip cuttings from non-flowering shoots in spring or summer.

H 45cm (18in)
S 30cm (12in)

15–17°C
(60–62°F)

Direct sunlight

Peperomia caperata
Emerald-ripple pepper

This is a small plant with heart-shaped, glossy, emerald green, deeply rippled leaves up to 3cm (1¼in) long. At the bottom of the ridges, the leaf looks almost black. The leaf petioles are green to dull red and up to 7.5cm (3in) long. *Peperomia caperata* 'Emerald Ripple' is a more compact plant with smaller leaves; *P. caperata* 'Little Fantasy' is a dwarf form.

Care
Keep the compost barely moist at all times. High humidity is important, but if the pot is standing on a tray of moist pebbles, make sure that the plant is set high and cannot take up the extra water. Feed with half-strength liquid fertilizer once a month in spring to autumn.

New plants
Take leaf cuttings in spring or summer. Use the whole leaf with 2.5cm (1in) of stalk attached, and insert it until the edge of the leaf is in contact with the compost.

Polystichum tsussimense
Holly fern, Korean rock fern

This is an evergreen fern from north-east Asia that grows into a shuttlecock-shaped plant, with broad, dark green fronds. Each frond is lance-shaped, with spiny-toothed and pointed pinnae. Ferns cannot thrive if they are neglected. They need both moist air and compost, while dry air, gas fumes and cold draughts will harm them, as well as allowing the compost to dry out and then soaking it.

Care
Keep moist, but do not allow compost to become waterlogged. This plant will benefit from monthly feeding throughout the growing season. Remove older fronds as their appearance deteriorates – a few at a time from right at their base in spring each year – to allow space for new shoots to develop.

New plants
Divide mature plants in spring, or break off new clumps from the rhizome with one or two fronds attached.

H 20cm (8in)
S 30cm (12in)

15–17°C
(60–62°F)

Partial shade

H 40cm (16in)
S 40cm (16in)

15–20°C
(60–70°F)

Partial shade

Senecio macroglossus

Natal ivy, Wax vine

This is a slender, twining plant bearing a strong resemblance to ivy but with softer, more fleshy, almost succulent-looking leaves. The stems and leaf stalks are purple and the leaves are mid-green. The form S. *macroglossus* 'Variegatus' is most commonly found; it is irregularly marked with cream, some shoots more than others – a few are almost entirely cream-coloured. Left to themselves, the stems will trail gracefully, making the plant a good subject for a hanging basket. Alternatively, it can be trained against a frame or thin stakes to give pretty, light-coloured height to an arrangement.

Care
Keep moist during spring to autumn. In winter, apply only sufficient water to prevent the compost drying out. Feed with standard liquid fertilizer every two weeks in spring to autumn. The small daisy-like flowers will only appear if the plant receives two to three hours of direct sunlight every day. If the shade is too deep, the cream variegations will begin to revert to green.

New plants
Take 7.5cm (3in) tip cuttings in spring or summer, and root in seed and cutting compost.

H To 2.1m (7ft)

15–20°C (60–70°F)

Partial shade

Stephanotis floribunda

Madagascar jasmine, Wax flower

This climbing shrub is best known for its heavily scented, waxy white flowers, but it also has wonderful leathery leaves of a glossy dark green. The 3cm (1¼ in) long flowers are produced in clusters of 10 or more, each being tubular in shape, flaring out into five lobes, and needs support as it grows. This plant will look equally attractive in a conservatory, trained against a wall or indoors on a small trellis or over an archway; take care to ensure it is positioned where its fragrance can be fully appreciated.

Care

Keep thoroughly moist from spring to autumn. In winter, apply only sufficient water to prevent the compost drying out. Set in a tray of pebbles to increase humidity, and mist daily if the temperature rises. Feed with standard liquid fertilizer every two weeks in spring to summer. Pinch out growing tips to encourage bushy growth.

New plants

Take tip cuttings and root in seed and cutting compost.

H To 3m (10ft)

15–20°C (60–70°F)

Partial shade

Aglaonema crispum

Painted drop tongue, Chinese evergreen

An attractive and long-lived plant, the aglaonema can eventually become a large specimen plant. The leaves are thick and leathery, growing to 30cm (12in) long and are olive in colour, edged with grey-green. The variety *A. crispum* 'Silver Queen' has dark grey-green leaves heavily marked with silvery white and cream. The flower is not particularly showy and consists of a spathe with a central spadix produced in summer or early autumn. As the plant ages, it tends to form a stout trunk, scarred by old leaf stalks, with a cluster of 10–15 leaves at the top. This can be disguised by grouping with other plants.

Care
Keep compost thoroughly moist during spring to autumn and slightly drier in winter. Feed with standard liquid fertilizer once a month in spring to summer.

New plants
With a sharp knife, sever a basal shot bearing three to four leaves and preferably some roots, at a point just below soil level in spring. Transplant and keep the pot enclosed in a plastic bag. Rooting should take six to eight weeks.

H To 90cm (36in)

15–20°C
(60–70°F)

Partial
shade

Alternanthera 'Purple Knight'

This is a striking plant grown for its impressive dark purple leaf colour. It is very tolerant, ideal for growing in a mixed container or display, where the dark foliage can be used to full effect on its own or as a foil among other plants. Its growth is fairly vigorous in the ground, but less so in a container, where the roots are more restricted. It has a branching, upright and spreading habit, which can be encouraged by regular pinching out while the plant is young. This plant will thrive in a hot summer.

Care
Keep the compost moist at all times but not wet, and give standard liquid fertilizer once a month during the growing season. Foliage colour is darkest in full sun.

New plants
Sow seed in a seed and cutting compost and cover with Vermiculite. Keep at 22–24°C (72–75°F) until germination in 3–5 days. Pot up quickly to allow individual plants room to branch.

Aloe vera
Aloe

Aloe vera has become popular since its increased use in medical preparations and because the direct application of juice from a snapped-off leaf is reputed to relieve the pain of a burn. Perhaps this is a plant everyone should keep at home. It grows as a rosette of grey-green succulent leaves, which are usually tinged red and are sometimes spotted. The edges of the leaves are pale pink and toothed. The flower spike grows to 90cm (36in), and the tubular yellow flowers are 3cm (1¼in) long.

Care
Water plentifully from spring until autumn, then sparingly in winter. Feed with full-strength liquid fertilizer every two weeks from spring until autumn. Check for pests regularly, because mealy bugs are inclined to hide in the folds of the rosette.

New plants
Detach suckers with a sharp knife, as close to the parent plant as possible, as soon as they begin to open into a rosette shape.

H 40–50cm (15–20in)
S 90cm (36in)

15–17°C (60–62°F)

Direct sunlight

H To 90cm (36in)

15–17°C (60–62°F)

Direct sunlight

Aphelandra squarrosa 'Louisiae'

Zebra plant, Saffron spike

This plant could be grown for its attractive foliage alone, so the bright yellow flower comes as a bonus. The leaves are a glossy dark green colour, with vivid white markings along the midrib and veins. They are 20–25cm (8–10in) long. The flowers – which are usually on the plant when it is purchased – are a brilliant golden yellow, and this earns the plant one of its common names. The actual flowers are fairly short-lived, but the surrounding bracts last long after the flowers have gone.

Care
Keep the compost thoroughly moist during spring to autumn. During winter the plant is resting, so allow the top half of the compost to dry between waterings. Aphelandras like high humidity, so set the pot in a tray of moist pebbles. Feed weekly with standard liquid fertilizer during spring and summer.

New plants
Take tip cuttings 10–15cm (4–6in) long during spring to summer. Root in seed and cutting compost in individual pots.

Caladium bicolor

Angel wings, Elephant's ear

The caladiums are a large group of tuberous-rooted plants with strikingly coloured, paper-thin, heart-shaped leaves that rise on long, fleshy stalks directly from the base. Leaf colour and size varies considerably between the different hybrids, and they look particularly attractive when they are grouped together or mixed with other foliage plants. *C. bicolor* 'White Queen' has white leaves with crimson veins and green edges; *C. bicolor* 'Carolyn Whorton' has pink leaves with green-black marbling and red ribs; *C. bicolor* 'Gingerland' has grey leaves with white ribs, maroon spots and dark green edges; and *C. bicolor* 'Miss Muffet' is a dwarf form, with sage-green leaves with white ribs and a soft red centre.

Care
Keep the compost thoroughly moist in spring to summer, but reduce watering through the rest period to a minimum just to prevent the compost from drying out. Feed with half-strength liquid fertilizer every two weeks during spring to summer. In order to thrive, caladiums need a five-month rest period starting when the leaves die down in autumn and lasting until the following spring.

New plants
As the plant emerges from its rest period, small tubers can be detached from the parent plant and potted on.

H 30–45cm (12–18in)

15–17°C (60–62°F)

Partial shade

H 60cm (24in)

18–23°C (65–75°F)

Partial shade

Chamaedorea elegans

Parlour palm

One of the most popular indoor palms, this plant has graceful, arching leaves that can grow up to 60cm (24in) in length from a short central stem. These darken from medium to glossy dark green as the plant ages, and the mature plant occasionally produces sprays of small yellow flowers. The variety *C. elegans* 'Bella' reaches to only half this height and is often the plant on sale for indoors.

Care

Keep compost thoroughly moist during spring to autumn, but during winter apply only sufficient water to prevent it from drying out. Humidity is important, so stand the pot on a tray of damp pebbles. Feed with half-strength liquid fertilizer once a month in spring to autumn.

New plants

It is not practical to take cuttings or grow from seed – buy small new plants instead.

Chrysalidocarpus lutescens

Areca palm, Yellow palm

The waxy stems of this dramatic palm grow in clusters, producing yellowish-green fronds that are first upright, then gradually arch over as the feathery green leaflets unfurl. Mature fronds can be up to 210cm (84in) long, with up to 60 leaflets on either side of the midrib. Growth is slow, with only about 20cm (8in) added each year to even the best-positioned plants. The remains of old fronds leave the stem marked like bamboo canes. This plant needs space but gives an instant jungle effect in a warm greenhouse or sunroom.

Care

Keep the soil thoroughly moist at all times, but reduce watering to a bare minimum if the temperature falls below 12°C (55°F). Feed with standard liquid fertilizer every two weeks from spring to autumn.

New plants

Remove suckers in spring, ideally about 30cm (12in) long with plenty of roots. Plant in free-draining compost.

H To 90cm (36in)

18–23°C (65–75°F)

Partial shade

H To 1.5m (5ft)

18–23°C (65–75°F)

Partial shade

Codiaeum variegatum var. pictum

Croton, Joseph's coat

The upward-pointing leaves of this tropical shrub are all glossy, leathery and heavily patterned but vary widely in their size, shape and colour. They can be long and thin or broad and rounded, straight or twisted, entire or lobed. As the plant ages, the colour of the leaves becomes more pronounced, in combinations of yellow, orange, pink and red with glossy dark green. Small, insignificant cream flowers are also produced as the plant ages.

Care

Keep the compost soil thoroughly moist during spring to autumn. In winter, apply only sufficient water to prevent it drying out. Increase humidity by standing the pot on a tray of moist pebbles. Feed with standard liquid fertilizer every two weeks in spring to autumn. The stems exude milky sap when cut, so if a large plant needs trimming back, do it in early spring and put a small piece of tissue over the cut to absorb the latex.

New plants

Take tip cuttings in spring or summer, and dip in rooting hormone before rooting in seed and cutting compost.

Ctenanthe oppenheimiana

Never-never plant

Ctenanthe is grown for its rosette of beautifully marked foliage rather than its insignificant white flowers. It is closely related to Maranta and Calathea, which are also grown for their leaves, but is more compact than either. A robust and bushy plant, it has leathery, lance-shaped leaves that grow to 45cm (18in) in length and are dark green with silvery grey feathering above and wine-red to purple below. The form *C. oppenheimiana* 'Tricolor' has leaves blotched with cream.

Care

Keep the compost moist during spring to autumn. In winter, apply only sufficient water to prevent it from drying out. Feed with standard liquid fertilizer every two weeks in spring to autumn. Increase humidity by standing the pot on a tray of moist pebbles.

New plants

Detach the basal offsets from the rhizomatous roots as close to the parent plant as possible, or take tip cuttings of three to four leaves. Plant in standard potting compost; with cuttings, use hormone rooting preparation and base heat, if possible.

H To 90cm (36in)

16–18°C (62–64°F)

Partial shade

H To 90cm (36in)

16–18°C (62–64°F)

Partial shade

Dieffenbachia maculata

Dumb cane

Grown for their decorative foliage, dieffenbachias make striking feature plants either on their own or in a massed arrangement. The large, downward-pointing leaves are soft and fleshy, and marked with white or cream in varying amounts according to the cultivar. The thick, woody, unbranched stem is inclined to become bare at the base as the plant ages. *Dieffenbachia maculata* 'Tropic White' is a form with large, blotched white leaves; *D. maculata* 'Veerie' has green-yellow leaves with white blotches. The common name is derived from the effect of the poisonous sap on the mouth and tongue – it causes painful swelling – so wash your hands thoroughly after touching this plant.

Care
Keep the compost moist at all times. Feed with standard liquid fertilizer every two weeks during spring to autumn.

New plants
Take tip cuttings 10–15cm (4–6in) long in spring, dip in rooting hormone, and keep warm (20°C/70°F) in a plastic bag or heated propagator. Alternatively, take a 10cm (4in) section of main stem with a growth bud and lay it horizontally on the potting compost and then treat it as a tip cutting.

Dracaena cincta 'Tricolor'

Rainbow plant

Dracaenas are shrubby plants, often resembling palms with their arching leaves and bare, woody stems. They are grown for the colour of their striking leaves, which are usually long and lance-shaped and striped or blotched with white, cream and/or red. The common name of this plant comes from the dramatic leaf colour. As the plant ages, the lower leaves turn down and fall, leaving the tuft of leaves atop a gradually lengthening, thin, bare stem.

Care
Keep the compost thoroughly moist during spring to autumn. In winter, apply only sufficient water to prevent it drying out. High humidity is important, so set the pot on a tray of moist pebbles. Feed with standard liquid fertilizer every two weeks from spring to autumn.

New plants
Take tip cuttings 10–15cm (4–6in) long from soft basal shoots in spring or early summer. Alternatively, longer pieces of mature woody stem can be inserted upright – the same way up as they were growing originally – into pots of seed and cutting compost to provide an instant 'tree' effect; or 5cm (2in) pieces of mature stem – each with at least one growth bud, a slight swelling under the bark – can be laid horizontally onto the compost, with the bud uppermost.

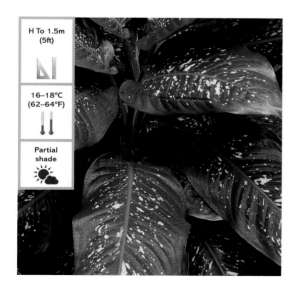

H To 1.5m (5ft)

16–18°C (62–64°F)

Partial shade

H To 1.5m (5ft)

16–25°C (62–80°F)

Partial shade

Dracaena fragrans
Deremensis group

The plants in this group have long, arching, lance-shaped leaves overlapping one another all the way up and around the stem. They are slow-growing and ultimately reach 120cm (48in) or more in height. *Dracaena fragrans* 'Lemon Lime' is a form with lime-green leaves that have pale yellow edges and a central stripe; *D. fragrans* 'Warneckei' features green leaves with two white stripes near the edge; and *D. fragrans* 'Yellow Stripe' has green leaves with rich yellow edges and a central stripe.

Care
Keep the compost thoroughly moist during spring to autumn. In winter, apply only sufficient water to prevent it drying out. High humidity is important, so stand the pot on a tray of moist pebbles. Feed with standard liquid fertilizer every two weeks from spring to autumn.

New plants
Take tip cuttings 10–15cm (4–6in) long from soft basal shoots in spring or early summer. Alternatively, longer pieces of mature woody stem can be inserted upright – the same way they were growing originally – into pots of seed and cutting compost to provide an instant 'tree' effect; or 5cm (2in) pieces of mature stem – each with at least one growth bud, a slight swelling under the bark – can be laid horizontally onto the compost, with the bud uppermost.

H To 1.2m (4ft)

16–25°C (62–80°F)

Partial shade

Elatostema repens var. *pulchrum*
Rainbow vine, Satin pellionia

A low, spreading plant, grown for its fleshy purple-tinted stems and striking leaves that are 2–5cm (1–2in) long. They are emerald green in colour, marked with a dull black-green along the midrib and veins above, and light purple below. This is a useful plant in a terrarium or bottle garden while it is small, or placed at the front of an arrangement to disguise the container and soften the outline, or in a hanging basket. As it grows, it will form roots wherever the stems are in contact with the compost.

Care
Keep the compost thoroughly moist during spring to autumn. In winter, apply only sufficient water to prevent it drying out. Feed with standard liquid fertilizer once a month in spring to summer. Mist occasionally in high temperatures, shelter from draughts, and do not allow direct sunlight to scorch the leaves.

New plants
Take tip cuttings in spring or summer, and root in seed and cutting compost. Lift layers at any time.

H To 45cm (18in)

16–25°C (62–80°F)

Partial shade

Epipremnum aureum
Devil's ivy, Golden pothos

The angular stems of this woody vine can be grown to either climb up a moist moss pole or cascade down from a high planter or hanging basket. They are striped with yellow or white and have aerial roots. The heart-shaped leaves are large, between 15–30cm (6–12in) long, and are green striped with yellow or white. *E. aureum* 'Marble Queen' has a white leaf stalk, green leaves streaked white and moss green, and white stems streaked with green. *E. aureum* 'Tricolor' has leaves boldly variegated in white and off-white stems and leaf stalks.

Care
Keep the compost moist during spring to autumn. In winter, apply only sufficient water to prevent it drying out. Feed with standard liquid fertilizer every two weeks in spring to summer. To maintain high humidity, place the pot on a tray of moist pebbles. Overwatering will cause root rot, and draughts will damage the foliage. Too little light will cause the leaf colours to revert to green.

New plants
Take tip cuttings 10cm (4in) long in spring or early summer, and root in seed and cutting compost.

Fittonia verschaffeltii var. argyroneura
Mosaic plant

Fittonias are creeping, stem-rooting evergreen plants that grow naturally in the warm, moist conditions of tropical rain forests. The downy leaves are 6–10cm (2½–4in) long, oval-shaped, and a deep olive-green with a dense network of coloured veins, carried on stems of 8cm (3¼in). The flowers are white, in slender four-angled spikes up to 8cm (3¼in) long, but they are largely concealed by bracts. The *verschaffeltii* species is an attractive small plant with rose-pink veins, so that the whole leaf is pink flushed. *F. verschaffeltii* var. *argyroneura* group, known as the silver net plant, has slightly larger leaves that are emerald green, closely net-veined with silver white.

Care
Careful watering is essential: too much, and the roots will rot; too little, and the leaves will shrivel and drop off. Keep barely moist at all times. Feed with half-strength liquid fertilizer every two weeks from spring to summer.

New plants
Take 5-cm (2-in)-long tip cuttings in spring or layer the plant by placing the pot inside a larger one filled with compost. Pin the tip of a shoot down onto the compost with a wire hoop until it roots; then gently sever it from the parent and transplant it.

H To 1.5m (5ft)

16–25°C (62–80°F)

Partial shade

15cm (6in)

18°C (65°F)

Partial shade

Grevillea robusta

Silky oak

With its graceful, 30cm (12in) long, arching foliage, this plant is an ideal mixer for a large arrangement. The leaves are bronze to dark green, ferny, and covered on the underside with silky hairs. It grows quickly, reaching 30cm (12in) in its first year, which makes a young plant a good subject for a table-top arrangement, and up to 1.8–2.1m (6–7ft) in four to five years, making it more useful in a large conservatory or greenhouse. The leaves tend to lose their ferny appearance as the plant ages, and it may be preferable to start again with a young plant after three to four years.

Care
Keep the compost moist from spring to autumn, but barely moist in winter. Feed with standard liquid fertilizer every two weeks during spring to summer.

New plants
Sow seed in ericaceous compost in spring or summer. Position in a bright spot, out of direct sunlight, at a temperature of 12–15°C (55–60°F).

Hedera helix

English ivy

The best-known of all the ivies, with a distinctive shape to the leaves, this is a bushy, densely leaved plant, ideal for trailing and groundcover. Within the grouping, there is a wide range of variations in colouring and leaf shape, although all are three- to five-lobed. The stems are stiff, but only self-supporting where the aerial roots can grip. They branch regularly, so the foliage fans out as it grows, and it can be used to trail from a shelf or from the front of a container to disguise it.

Care
Keep compost moist from spring to autumn, but apply only sufficient water to prevent it drying out in winter. In high temperatures, increase the humidity by misting or standing the pot on a tray of moist pebbles. Feed with standard liquid fertilizer every two weeks from spring to autumn. Variegated plants will lose their leaf markings if they are placed in too dark a location.

New plants
Propagation can be done by layering. Otherwise, take tip cuttings and root them in water or potting compost.

H 1.8–2.1m
(6–7ft)

16–25°C
(62–80°F)

Direct
sunlight

H 90cm
(36in)

16–25°C
(62–80°F)

Partial
shade

Howea forsteriana
Kentia palm

This is a tolerant palm that seems to thrive in a range of indoor conditions. It makes a lovely specimen plant, particularly as it grows taller, but it needs plenty of room to grow well. The graceful, dark green foliage is almost flat in appearance, borne on tall, straight leaf stalks, with the many long leaflets drooping only slightly on each side of the raised midrib.

Care
Keep the compost thoroughly moist from spring to autumn. In winter, apply only sufficient water to prevent it drying out. Water with standard liquid fertilizer once a month from spring to autumn. Wipe the leaves periodically with tepid water to remove dust.

New plants
Sow fresh seed – which is rarely produced on indoor plants – at a temperature of 25°C (80°F).

Hypoestes phyllostachya
Polka-dot plant

Grown for their unusual foliage, these are small, shrub-like plants that are usually grown for a year and then discarded when they grow too tall and woody. When they are young, the foliage is bushy, and the leaves are dark or olive green, conspicuously spotted with pink. Small lilac-coloured flowers may be produced in spring, which will take energy from the leaves, so they may be pinched out.

Care
Keep the compost moist from spring to autumn. In winter, apply only sufficient water to prevent it drying out. Feed with standard liquid fertilizer every two weeks during spring to autumn. Keep in a well-lit area because too little light will cause the pink markings to become green.

New plants
Sow seed in spring or take 10cm (4in) tip cuttings in spring to summer. Root in seed and cutting compost, and keep damp but not wet.

H 2.4m (8ft)

16–25°C (62–80°F)

Partial shade

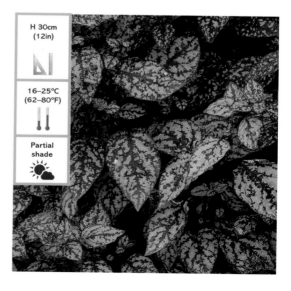

H 30cm (12in)

16–25°C (62–80°F)

Partial shade

Maranta leuconeura
Prayer plant

The common name of this plant is derived from its habit of folding its leaves together at night. It is grown primarily for its striking foliage. The leaves are oval shaped, up to 12.5cm (5in) long, and a lustrous dark green, marked with grey or maroon, and veined silver, red or purple above and grey-green or maroon below. The white or violet flowers are small and insignificant. *Maranta leuconeura* 'Erythroneura' – known as the herringbone plant – has green-black leaves with scarlet veins and a lime-green zone along the midrib. *M. leuconeura* 'Kerchoveana' – Rabbit's foot – has grey-green leaves with a row of purple-brown to olive blotches along each side of the midrib.

Care
Keep the compost thoroughly moist in spring to autumn and drier in winter. Feed with standard liquid fertilizer once a month during spring to summer. Do not allow water to splash onto the leaves or it will cause discoloration.

New plants
Divide large clumps in spring, or take 10cm (4in) long cuttings with three to four leaves in spring or summer. Root in seed and cutting compost.

Monstera deliciosa
Swiss cheese plant

In its native habitat, the monstera will scramble up the trunks and along the branches of large trees, anchoring itself in place by means of strong aerial roots, which also serve to take in moisture and nutrients. It matures into a large plant, with heart-shaped leaves up to 45cm (18in) across on 30cm (12in) stalks. The common name arises from the leaves, which are undivided on a young plant but gradually become deeply incised between the veins, with holes in the remaining sections.

Care
Keep barely moist all year round. Train the stem against a moss pole to allow the aerial roots to anchor and take in moisture as they would in the wild. Feed with standard liquid fertilizer once a month from spring to autumn.

New plants
Take tip cuttings of two leaves in spring or stem cuttings of a single node with a short length of stem, layer or air layer.

H 30cm
(12in)

16–25°C
(62–80°F)

Partial
shade

H 3m
(10ft)

16–25°C
(62–80°F)

Partial
shade

Nephrolepsis exaltata '**Bostoniensis**'

Boston fern

This is a lush, graceful fern with long, arching fronds and makes a lovely specimen plant on a pedestal or in a hanging basket. In the right conditions, the fronds can reach 120cm (48in) long, and are a rich mid-green, with numerous pinnae occurring alternately on each side of the midrib. Rows of brown sporangia – which produce spores, the equivalent of seeds – develop on the undersides of the fronds.

Care

Keep the compost thoroughly moist at all times. In higher temperatures, dry air will cause browning of the pinnae, so be sure to increase humidity by standing the pot on a tray of moist pebbles. Feed with standard liquid fertilizer every two weeks from spring to autumn.

New plants

Furry runners grow from the rhizome, and plantlets develop at their tips. Remove the plantlet once it has rooted by severing the runner with a sharp knife. Spore propagation is not easy, because viability is variable..

Nerium oleander

Oleander

A large evergreen shrub with leathery, dark green leaves, this is grown for its display of beautiful, often fragrant, funnel-shaped flowers. These are produced in terminal clusters and can be single, semi-double or fully double, according to the variety, in shades of white, cream, yellow, apricot, salmon, copper, pink, red, carmine and purple. Individual flowers can be up to 5cm (2in) across, and they are borne in groups of six to eight. This is an ideal plant for a sunny windowsill while it is small and for a well-lit greenhouse as it grows. The whole plant is poisonous (sap, flowers and seeds), so handle with extreme caution and wash thoroughly after contact.

Care

Keep the compost thoroughly moist from spring to autumn, but barely moist in winter. Allowing the plant to dry out as the flowers form will result in the buds being shed. Feed with standard liquid fertilizer every two weeks during spring to summer. Keep at normal room temperature from spring to autumn but below 15°C (60°F) and above 7°C (45°F) in winter for the rest period.

New plants

Take tip cuttings up to 15cm (6in) long in summer, and root them in water or potting compost.

H 45cm (18in)
S 90cm (36in)

16–25°C (62–80°F)

Partial shade

H To 1.8m (6ft

16–25°C (62–80°F)

Direct sunlight

Pteris cretica

Table fern, Cretan brake

This is a neat, small fern that forms a clump of fronds from a short underground rhizome. Each frond has a slender stalk 20–25cm (8–10in) long, and arching leaflets, which can be striped, variegated or plain, according to the variety, and carried singly or in forked pairs. *Pteris cretica albolineata* has leaf segments with a broad white stripe; *P. cretica* 'Parkeri' is a larger plant, with glossy fronds and finely toothed leaflets. *P. cretica* 'Rivertoniana' has deeply lobed leaves and leaflets in four or five pairs.

Care
Keep the compost thoroughly moist at all times. In higher temperatures, increase the humidity by setting the pot on a tray of moist pebbles. Feed with half-strength liquid fertilizer once a month in spring to autumn. Cut out older fronds as they fade to make room for new ones.

New plants
Divide larger plants in spring or propagate from spores.

H 30cm (12in)

15–20°C
(60–70°F)

Partial
shade

Sansevieria trifasciata

Mother-in-law's tongue, Snake plant

This is one plant that seems to survive when no others can. It is tolerant of sunshine and shade, dry air, draughts, and even a certain amount of neglect in terms of watering. Each rhizomatous plant can last many years, because the rate of growth is slow, and they seldom need repotting. The leaves are narrow, flat, long and pointed, held stiffly erect and banded light and dark green. *Sansevieria trifasciata* 'Laurentii' is a form in which the leaf margins are bright yellow, while *S. trifasciata* 'Golden Hahnii' has leaves that form a squat rosette and are banded grey with cream margins.

Care
Keep the compost moist during spring to autumn. In winter, apply only sufficient water to prevent it drying out. Feed with half-strength liquid fertilizer once a month in spring to summer. Sansevierias grow best when slightly pot-bound, so do not repot each year.

New plants
Divide clumps of the mature plant so that each new piece has both leaves and roots, or take leaf cuttings by clipping one leaf into short pieces and inserting them base-downward into a pot or tray of potting compost. Because the yellow part of the variegated leaf contains no chlorophyll and cannot produce roots, plants propagated by leaf cuttings will be green only.

Saxifraga stolonifera

Mother of thousands, Strawberry geranium

This is a small evergreen plant that spreads by means of long, thin, red stolons, which bear plantlets at their tips. The common name 'mother of thousands' arises from the copious quantities of these small plants that are produced. The round, bristly, long-stalked leaves are rosette- or tuft-forming, mid-green with silvery veins above and flushed red beneath. Branched flowering stems up to 40cm (15in) long are produced in late summer and early autumn, bearing clusters of white flowers. *Saxifraga stolonifera* 'Tricolor' is less vigorous and has leaves edged cream with a pink flush. It needs a normal room temperature, rather than cool, with direct sunlight for at least part of each day to ensure good coloration.

Care
Keep the compost thoroughly moist in spring to autumn. In winter, apply only sufficient water to prevent it drying out. In higher temperatures, increase the humidity using a tray of moist pebbles, but do not allow to stand in water or the roots will rot. Feed with standard liquid fertilizer once a month during spring to summer.

New plants
Root the plantlets into small pots of potting compost, either before or after detaching from the parent plant.

H 60cm (24in)

16–25°C (62–80°F)

Partial shade

H 20cm (8in)

15–17°C (60–62°F)

Partial shade

Schefflera actinophylla
Umbrella tree

In its native habitat, this plant can become a tree up to 12m (40ft) high, but indoors it is more usual to see it as a pretty, bushy shrub, with leaves borne in terminal rosettes resembling the spokes of an umbrella, hence the common name. The upright petioles can reach as long as 80cm (33in), each bearing seven to 16 glossy, bright green leaflets that grow to 30x10cm (12x4in). Schefflera will look equally attractive grown as individual specimens or used in a group display, where the lush foliage softens outlines and acts as a foil for brighter-coloured leaves or flowers.

Care
Keep the compost moist in spring to autumn. In winter, apply only sufficient water to prevent it drying out. Increase humidity by setting the pot on a tray of moist pebbles and misting when temperatures are high. Feed with standard liquid fertilizer once a month during spring to autumn.

New plants
Take tip cuttings in summer, use rooting hormone and seal the pot plus cuttings in a plastic bag at 21°C (70°F).

Tolmeia menziesii
Pickaback plant, Mother of thousands

The pickaback plant is so-called because of the way in which the young plants develop on the older leaves at the point where the leaf joins the petiole. The weight of these new plants pulls the leaves down so that they trail and look attractive in a hanging basket. The foliage is lime-green and covered with fine hairs, giving it a downy appearance. Small greenish white flowers are produced in late spring to early summer.

Care
Keep moist in spring to autumn. In winter, apply only sufficient water to prevent the compost drying out. Feed with standard liquid fertilizer every two weeks during spring to summer. If a tolmiea outgrows its allotted space, it can be planted outdoors and replaced indoors by a young plantlet.

New plants
Use well-developed plantlets, and either peg them down into a pot of compost or detach and push the leaf stalk into the compost to keep the leaf in good contact with it.

H To 2.1m (7ft)

16–25°C (62–80°F)

Partial shade

H 30cm (12in)

15–17°C (60–62°F)

Partial shade

X *Fatshedera lizei*

Ivy tree

The result of a breeding cross between two distinct genera within the same plant family – denoted by the x *Fatshedera* before the name. In this case, the result is an attractive evergreen plant bearing characteristics of both parents, and the general ease of cultivation of both. From *Fatsia* come the wide-spreading glossy leaves, from *Hedera* the sprawling stems, which can easily be trained up canes or pinched out to produce a more bushy effect. The young leaves are covered in rust-coloured hairs. x *F. lizei* 'Pia' has wavy green leaves; x *F. lizei* 'Annemieke' has leaves marked with yellow and x *F. lizei* 'Variegata' has leaves with white markings.

Care

Keep the compost moist from spring to autumn, but apply only sufficient water in winter to prevent it drying out. In warmer locations, increase humidity by standing the pot on a tray of moist pebbles. Feed with standard liquid fertilizer every two weeks during spring to summer. Keep variegated forms above 15°C (60°F) at all times.

New plants

Take tip cuttings 10cm (4in) long, or stem cuttings 5cm (2in) long, in spring to summer. Dip in rooting hormone and enclose in a plastic bag. Place in a warm, bright location.

H 1.2m (4ft)

15–20°C (60–70°F)

Partial shade

Aspidistra elatior
Cast-iron plant

The aspidistra is one of the most resilient houseplants ever introduced. It is tolerant of bad light, gas fumes – hence its popularity in Victorian times – and even extreme temperatures. It grows as a clump, producing many single dark green leaves that reach lengths of up to 60cm (24in). The cream and purple flowers are produced in spring and are 2.5cm (1in) long, but may not be seen among the foliage.

Other forms include A. elatior 'Milky Way', which has leaves speckled with white; A. elatior 'Variegata', with variegated cream leaves, and A. elatior 'Variegata Exotica', which has leaves very boldly streaked with white.

Care
Aim to keep the compost barely moist at all times. Overwatering causes brown blotches on the surface of the leaves. Feed with standard liquid fertilizer at each watering.

New plants
Divide large plants in spring; each piece should have both leaves and some roots. Plant in a humus-rich compost in individual pots.

Asplenium nidus
Bird's nest fern

This true fern takes its common name from the arrangement of its leathery, apple-green leaves, which form an open rosette. Unlike many ferns, the leaves are uncut and may reach 120cm (48in) in length – although they are usually about 45cm (18in) long by 5–7.5cm (2–3 in) wide. New leaves uncurl from the central, fibrous brown core, and for the first few weeks they are quite delicate, so they should not be handled. Brown blotches on the reverse of older fronds are likely to be spore cases rather than insects, particularly if they are arranged in a regular pattern.

Care
Keep the compost thoroughly moist. Mature fronds will benefit from having dust gently wiped away at regular intervals. Feed with standard liquid fertilizer once a month during spring to autumn.

New plants
Propagation is by spores – which is difficult to achieve. Offsets are not formed.

H 45cm (18in)

15–17°C (60–62°F)

Partial shade

H 60cm (24in)

15–17°C (60–62°F)

Partial shade

Fatsia japonica
Japanese fatsia

This is a wide-spreading evergreen shrub that can be grown indoors or out. It has large, leathery, many fingered leaves that leave prominent scars on the woody stem as they fall. Fatsia makes an impressive specimen plant, but it grows quickly and needs plenty of room. The foliage tends to be a lighter colour indoors than outdoors, and the creamy white flowers will be produced only on a mature plant that is kept in cool conditions.

Care
Keep the compost thoroughly moist from spring to autumn, but just moist in winter. Feed with standard liquid fertilizer every two weeks during spring to autumn. Large plants can be pruned hard in spring to remove up to half the growth.

New plants
Take stem cuttings 5cm (2in) long during spring to summer, remove the lower leaves, and dip the end in rooting hormone. Enclose in a plastic bag or propagation case at around 15°C (60°F) in a well-lit position.

Philidendron bipinnatifidum
Tree philodendron

This is a tree-like shrub, usually with a single, sturdy, upright stem that is inclined to fall over and lie horizontally as it ages, with just the tip pointing upwards. The downward-pointing leaves grow to 100cm (39in) in length, half of which is the leaf stalk. They are heart-shaped, bright green and deeply cut, with many narrow, wavy-edged lobes. The flower is a spathe 30cm (12in) long and cream with a red margin. *Philodendron bipinnatifidum* 'German Selloum' is a form with finely cut leaves and wavy, graceful lobes; *P. bipinnatifidum* 'Miniature Selloum' is a dwarf form, with small leaves and thick petioles; *P. bipinnatifidum* 'Variegatum' has leaves blotched light green to yellow.

Care
Keep moist from spring to autumn. In winter, apply only sufficient water to prevent the compost drying out. Feed with standard liquid fertilizer once a month in spring to summer. Variegated plants always need more light than green forms; the plant will compensate for the low light by converting the yellow leaf areas to green, and the markings will fade or be lost altogether.

New plants
Sow fresh seed in spring, or take tip cuttings from shoots at the base of the plant.

H 1.5m (5ft)

7–15°C (45–60°F)

Partial shade

H To 5m (15ft)

15–17°C (60–62°F)

Partial shade

Ananus bracteatus var. tricolor

Red pineapple

Pineapples ultimately grow into very large plants, so they are only suitable for use indoors for a few years. In a heated greenhouse, they will last until they outgrow their allotted space. They are dramatic plants with rosettes of long, sharply toothed leaves striped with cream and flushed and edged with pink. The fruit forms on a 30–45cm (12–18in) long stalk and is green-brown in colour surrounded by red bracts. Unless the growing conditions are ideal, it may not be edible.

Care

Keep the compost moist at all times, but not wet. Pineapples like high humidity, so stand the pot on a tray of damp pebbles and mist regularly. Feed with standard liquid fertilizer at every watering.

New plants

Detach offsets when they are 10–15cm (4–6in) long, and pot up in seed and cutting compost. Rooting should take about eight weeks.

Calathea makoyana

Peacock plant, Cathedral windows, Brain plant

Although this tropical plant produces white flowers surrounded by green bracts, they are of minor importance compared to the dramatic foliage. The oval-shaped leaves can be as long as 33cm (13in) and are a pale green in colour, and feathered cream with dark green blotches along the veins, with a dark green edge. Underneath, they have the same pattern, but it is shaded with purple.

Care

Keep the compost thoroughly moist in spring to autumn and slightly drier in winter. In warmer temperatures, increase the humidity by misting daily with rainwater, to avoid marking the foliage. Bright light will cause the leaf markings to fade. Feed with standard liquid fertilizer every two weeks in spring to summer.

New plants

Divide mature plants in spring; each clump needs roots and shoots to grow. Enclose the new plant in a plastic bag after potting up to keep the humidity high until it has rooted.

H 90cm (36in)

15–17°C (60–62°F)

Direct sunlight

H 100cm (39in)

15–20°C (60–70°F)

Partial shade

Chlorophytum comosum
Spider plant, Ribbon plant

The half-hardy spider plant is a dramatic trailing plant when set in a hanging basket or in a container on a pedestal, where it can grow unhindered. This effect is enhanced by the long, curved, straplike leaves, and arching stems bearing tiny white flowers or numerous small plantlets. *C. comosum* 'Vittatum' has green leaves with a broad white stripe running lengthwise down the centre. *C. comosum* 'Picturatum' has a yellow central stripe, and *C. comosum* 'Variegatum' is green at the centre and white or cream at the edges.

Care
Keep the compost thoroughly moist during spring to autumn but slightly drier in winter. Allowing the plant to dry out will result in permanent brown tips on the leaves. Feed with standard liquid fertilizer every two weeks from spring to autumn.

New plants
Young plantlets can be rooted in water or seed and cutting compost either before or after being detached from the parent. If they are in water, transplant as soon as the roots are 2.5cm (1in) long.

Cocos nucifera
Coconut palm

The coconut palm makes an interesting and unusual feature plant, either growing alone as a specimen or as a high point in a grouping. The trunk grows directly from the nut itself, which is partially buried in the compost, and the arching fronds have a sheath of woven, light brown fibres.

Care
Keep the compost moist at all times, and feed with half-strength liquid fertilizer every two weeks during spring to summer. This plant has a limited life in the home because it resents root disturbance and, to grow well, it needs intense heat and high humidity, which is difficult to maintain.

New plants
Propagation of this plant is almost impossible to achieve at home.

H 60cm (24in)
S 60cm (24in)

16–18°C
(62–64°F)

Partial shade

H To 3m
(10ft)

15–25°C
(60–80°F)

Partial shade

Dionaea muscipula
Venus flytrap

In its natural environment, this carnivorous plant needs to supplement its nutrient intake by trapping insects and digesting their contents, and it has evolved a mechanism for catching them that makes it a fascinating plant to watch. It grows as a low rosette of leaves that have a broadly winged, leafy petiole and two rounded, hinged blades that become a glossy, bright red in sunlight and are fringed with spines. When a fly triggers the reaction, the leaves snap shut on the prey. These plants are not normally very long-lived in the home but are an interesting addition while they last.

Care
Keep the compost thoroughly moist at all times. Feed with extra flies or tiny pieces of meat occasionally.

New plants
These are bought as small plants and cannot be propagated in the home.

Echeveria agavoides
Echeveria

Fleshy, triangular mid-green leaves are arranged in a rosette around the short stem. They are sharply pointed and waxy, with transparent margins. The flower head is double-branched, with small flowers that open successively from the base of the curled spike towards the tip. Each is bell-shaped, pink-orange outside, yellow within, and about 12mm (½in) across. If the plant is grown in full sunlight, the edges of the leaves will take on a reddish tint. *Echeveria agavoides* 'Metallica' has purple-lilac leaves, turning olive-bronze.

Care
Keep the compost barely moist at all times. Overwatering to even a small extent will cause soft growth that is liable to rot. Feed with standard liquid fertilizer once a month during spring to autumn. Keep the plant at a winter temperature of 12–15°C (55–60°F) for the winter rest.

New plants
Take leaf cuttings or remove offsets, and root in seed and cutting compost.

H 45cm
(18in)

20–25°C
(70–80°F)

Direct
sunlight

H 15cm
(6in)

15–17°C
(60–62°F)

Direct
sunlight

Ficus elastica
Rubber plant

This is the original rubber plant that has been popular as an indoor plant for many years, although it has been largely superseded by a number of newer cultivars with a more compact habit or coloured leaf markings. The glossy leaves are large and leathery, with a prominent midrib and a pointed tip. They arise from a single tall stem, which rarely produces side shoots unless the top is removed. *Ficus elastica* 'Robusta' has rather larger and wider leaves, in *F. elastica* 'Decora' the leaves are broad and shiny with a white midrib; *F. elastica* 'Tricolor' has grey-green leaves that are variegated pink and cream; and *F. elastica* 'Variegata' has pale green leaves with a white or yellow margin.

Care
Keep compost thoroughly moist at all times, but not wet. Apply standard liquid fertilizer once a month in spring to autumn.

New plants
Take tip cuttings 10cm (4in) long in spring. The cutting will root better if the bottom 12mm (½in) has become light brown and woody. To prevent the latex from forming a cap on the base of the cutting, strip the leaves from the lower third and place it in water for 30 minutes. Remove, shake off the water, and dip only the cut surface in rooting hormone, then pot up in seed and cutting compost and seal in a plastic bag in a bright place, out of direct sun.

Epiphyllum crenatum
Orchid cactus

This vigorous, bushy, semi-epiphytic cactus has an upright habit with a cylindrical main stem and leaf-like, grey-green branches. These have a wavy, toothed edging and are up to 12.5cm (5in) wide. The striking, fragrant, funnel-shaped flowers are creamy white, with green, pink or pale yellow outer segments, and may be up to 20cm (8in) long. They are produced in summer and last for two to three days but are diurnal – they open during the day and close again at night.

Care
Water freely from spring until autumn; then apply only enough water to prevent the compost drying out. This cactus likes high humidity, so mist regularly or stand the pot on a saucer of pebbles and keep the water level high enough to evaporate around the foliage. Feed with liquid tomato fertilizer at half-strength every two weeks from spring to late summer.

New plants
Take stem cuttings in spring, and root in seed and cutting compost.

H 1.8m (6ft)

15–17°C (60–62°F)

Partial shade

H 90cm (36in)
S 90cm (36in)

15–17°C (60–62°F)

Partial shade

Outdoor Plants

Abutilon x *hybridum* 'Bella Vanilla'
Flowering maple

This is a striking half-hardy flowering plant that can be raised quite easily from seed. It will flower during its first season, producing large, open, bell-shaped blooms approximately 7.5cm (3in) in diameter, with a large golden central stamen. Each flower lasts only about two days, but each is produced in succession. The plant will tolerate bright sun or partial shade and is happy in a range of temperatures, although the flower colour tends to be slightly better in cooler temperatures. The wide, light green leaves are smaller than most other abutilons, making the flowers seem even larger.

Care
Keep the compost moist at all times and use standard liquid fertilizer every two weeks during the flowering season.

New plants
Sow seed in sterile seed and cutting compost. Keep at 22–24°C (72–75°F) until germination, which should be in 3–5 days. Pot up the seedlings quickly to allow each plant room to branch. From sowing to first flowering should only be about 12 weeks.

H 45cm (18in)
S 30cm (12in)

16–18°C
(62–64°F)

Direct
sunlight

Anemone blanda
Anemone

This is a charming, clump-forming hardy perennial with comparatively large, saucer-shaped, deep purple-blue flowers in spring. The mainly basal leaves are divided into three mid- to deep green, irregularly lobed and toothed leaflets. Grow in ordinary, ideally humus-rich soil in sun or partial shade. Propagate by dividing the tubers when dormant. *A. b.* 'Atrocaerulea' is deep blue, *A. b.* 'Charmer', deep pink, and *A. b.* 'White Splendour' has large, white flowers. *A. nemorosa*, Wood Anemone, with white, often pink-backed or blue flowers, is similar but spreads more widely. *A. ranunculoides* is similar in habit but has bright yellow, single or double flowers. *A. coronaria* has showy, single flowers in red, blue or white in spring.

Care
Keep soil moist during the growing season. The plant will die back completely by summer, so be careful not to damage the tubers when digging, as it can be easy to forget about dormant plants when later things are in full flower.

New plants
By division in spring, or by fresh seed sown in late summer. Root cuttings can also be taken in winter. The plant may also self-seed or be spread by bird-deposited seed.

Browallia speciosa
Bush violet

A glorious display of large sapphire blue flowers in autumn and winter makes browallia an impressive and attractive potted plant. The trailing stems lend themselves to use in a hanging basket and by removing the flowers as they fade, the display can be prolonged for several weeks. It is best treated as a half-hardy annual and discarded once flowering is over. *B. speciosa* 'Major' has a more upright habit, bright green leaves and large violet-blue flowers with a white throat and deep blue veining on the petals. *B. speciosa* 'Silver Bells' is a white form.

Care
Keep the compost moist at all times. Feed with standard liquid fertilizer every two weeks while the plant is in flower. The thin branches need tying to stakes if the plant is to be grown as a bush. Higher than recommended temperatures will make the flowers fade quickly.

New plants
Sow seed in seed and cutting compost in spring or summer. Pinch out the tips of the shoots as they grow to make them bushy.

H 15cm (6in)
S 15cm(6in)

13–16°C
(55–62°F)

Direct
sunlight

H To 60cm
(24in)
S 25cm(10in)

13–16°C
(55–62°F)

Direct
sunlight

Brugmansia x candida

This is a spectacular shrub, also known as Angel's Trumpet, with robust, sparingly branched stems and large, oval to elliptic, sometimes toothed, mid- to deep green leaves. The 25–30cm (10–12in) long, pendant, trumpet-shaped flowers are white to soft yellow, or (rarely) pink, from summer to autumn. Grow in fertile, moist but well-drained soil in sun or partial shade. Propagate by semihardwood cuttings in summer. *B. x c.* 'Grand Marnier' has apricot flowers. *B. x c.* 'Knightii' has semidouble, white ones.

Care
Grow this half-hardy shrub outdoors in moist, but well-drained, soil in a sheltered, frost-free area in full sun. Alternatively, grow under glass indoors, in loam-based compost.

New plants
Propagate from either seed or semi-hardwood cuttings.

H 3–5m (10–15ft)
S 1.5–2.5m (5–8ft)

13–16°C
(55–62°F)

Direct
sunlight

Camellia japonica
Camellia

Camellias are hardy large shrubs or small trees that will survive all but the very harshest winters outdoors, as long as they are growing in the acid conditions they prefer. They can be grown under cover, where they will benefit from protection against the weather, but they need a cool, light, airy position, such as an unheated greenhouse. The leaves are a glossy dark green, and the flowers come in a range of colours from white to dark red. Varieties are available with single, semi-double and double flowers, produced from late winter until summer, according to variety.

Care
Keep the compost thoroughly moist at all times and feed with standard liquid fertilizer every two weeks during spring to summer.

New plants
Take semi-ripe cuttings in summer, with at least 2.5cm (1in) of brown, woody stem at the base. They will need rooting hormone and bottom heat – an electric propagator would be ideal.

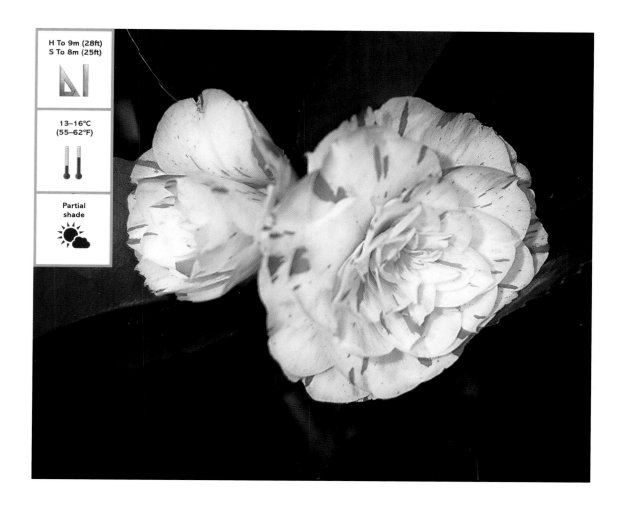

H To 9m (28ft)
S To 8m (25ft)

13–16°C
(55–62°F)

Partial shade

Canna x generalis

Canna lily

Cannas have tall, erect flower spikes carrying exotic blooms that come in a wide variety of colours ranging from white to red through yellow and pink. They can be plain, striped or spotted. This half-hardy plant makes a bold, cheerful addition to a display, particularly in a warm position. The leaves, arising from the rhizomatous root system, are long and straplike, ranging from grey and leathery to chocolate red and thin. *C.* x *generalis* 'Black Knight' has brown leaves and red flowers, *C.* x *generalis* 'Lucifer' is a dwarf form with green leaves and crimson flowers with yellow borders, and *C.* x *generalis* 'Orchid' has deep pink flowers.

Care
Keep the compost thoroughly moist during spring to autumn, but reduce watering through the winter to a minimum just to prevent the mix from drying out. Feed with standard liquid fertilizer every two weeks from summer to autumn. If the temperature is very high, mist regularly. Overwinter in a frost-free place, ideally indoors.

New plants
Divide the rhizomes in spring and transplant individually.

H To 1.5m (5ft)
S To 50cm (20in)

16–18°C
(62–64°F)

Direct
sunlight

Colchicum speciosum
Autumn crocus

Indispensable for the autumn garden, hardy autumn crocus produces sturdy, goblet-shaped flowers up to 20cm (8in) long in shades of pale to deep rose-purple, often with white throats before the leaves. The spring-maturing leaves are glossy mid- to deep green, lance-shaped to oblong, in sheafs of three or four, fading by mid-summer. Grow in moist, well-drained soil in sun or partial shade. Propagate by removing offsets when dormant. *C. s.* 'Album' has shapely, pure white, firm-textured flowers. Several cultivars are derived from this species, like 'The Giant' with larger, violet-purple flowers and 'Waterlily' which has fully double, lilac-pink flowers.

Care
This plant grows best in partial sun, since it will fade and burn in full sun. It prefers moisture during the leaf expanding stage of growth.

New plants
Separate corms when they are dormant in the summer months.

H 15cm (6in)
S 10cm (4in)

13–16°C
(55–62°F)

Partial
shade

Crocus spp.
Crocus

Crocus corms are generally known as bulbs but they are actually solid stems from which a bud containing the leaves and flower emerges. These hardy plants are normally associated with springtime in the garden, but there are a number of varieties that will grow very well before then, giving colour in the early months of the year when there is little else around. These include the smaller-flowered *C. chrysanthus*, which flowers in January to February; the slightly later *C. vernus*, flowering in February; and the large-flowered Dutch hybrids, which flower February to March. The cup-shaped flowers come in a variety of colours, including purple, yellow and white, and can be plain or striped. All have long, thin, green-and-white striped leaves.

Care
Keep the compost moist but not too wet. It is not necessary to feed; once the flowers begin to fade, remove just the flowers and continue watering, leaving the stem and leaves to die down gradually.

New plants
Unlike bulbs, corms do not flower a second time, but produce new corms from lateral buds. These can be detached and transplanted.

H 8cm (3in)
S 5cm (2in)

13–16°C
(55–62°F)

Direct sunlight

Dahlia hybrida 'Dahlietta'
Pot dahlia

This is a new collection of small forms of the popular garden dahlia, ideal for bringing colour to container displays during the summer months. They are half-hardy, generally easy to grow, form neat, compact plants, and will flower profusely. The lush foliage is mid-green or bronze, according to the variety, and the large, fully double flowers come in white and shades of pink, red, orange and yellow. The Surprise series all have petals marked with secondary colours as flecks, splashes, brushstrokes or picotee edging.

Care
Keep the compost moist at all times. Feed with liquid fertilizer at half strength every two weeks while flowering. Pinching out the very tip from one or two young shoots will encourage basal branching and build a stronger plant. Overwinter in a frost-free place, ideally indoors.

New plants
Take tip cuttings in spring and root at 20–23°C (68–74°F).

H 22cm (9in)
S 40cm (16in)

16–18°C
(62–64°F)

Direct sunlight

Dianthus 'Dynasty'

Sweet William

This impressive new series of F1 introductions (a Sweet William cross hybrid) is unusual in that it does not require a period of winter cold to promote flowering, so the plants will grow well and flower in warmer conditions. They will grow quickly to fill a container and will flower throughout the spring, summer and autumn. Each has lightly scented, double flowers that resemble tiny carnations. They are well branched and upright, and the profuse flowers last well if they are cut for the vase. Flower colours include purple, red, white and rose with a white picotee edging.

Care
Keep the compost moist at all times. Feed with liquid fertilizer at half strength every two weeks. These are hardy but not long-lived plants.

New plants
Plants have to be bought because seed seldom sets and does not grow true to type.

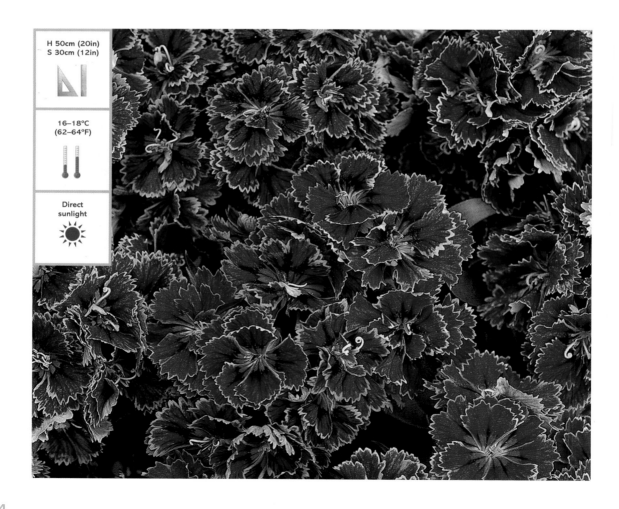

H 50cm (20in)
S 30cm (12in)

16–18°C
(62–64°F)

Direct
sunlight

Diascia rigescens
Diascia

This is a delightful, bushy, erect to spreading, evergreen, half-hardy perennial with angular stems and heartshaped, toothed, mid- to deep green leaves. Rich pink flowers are carried in dense, erect spikes through summer and add useful decoration to containers. *D. barberae* 'Ruby Field' is mat forming, with heartshaped leaves and salmon-pink flowers. *D. b.* 'Blackthorn Apricot' is similar with apricot flowers. *D. rigescens* 'Lilac Belle' is more compact with lilac-pink flowers.

Care
Grow in fertile, well-drained soil in full sun.

New plants
Propagate by softwood cuttings in spring or late summer. Overwinter in a frost-free place, ideally indoors.

H 45cm (18in)
S 45cm (18in)

16–18°C
(62–64°F)

Direct
sunlight

Felicia amelloides
Felicia

This is a dainty, bushy, half-hardy semishrub with oval to narrowly spoon-shaped, deep green leaves and bright blue, yellow-centred, daisy flowers from summer to autumn. *F. a.* 'Read's Blue' is rich blue, *F. a.* 'Read's White' is white, and *F. a.* 'Santa Anita Variegated' has white-patterned leaves. These plants make a delightful addition to containers of all sizes and mix well with a wide variety of other plants.

Care
Grow in well-drained soil in direct sunlight. Overwinter in a frost-free place, ideally indoors.

New plants
Propagate by seed in spring or softwood cuttings in summer.

H 30cm (12in)
S 30cm (12in)

16–18°C
(62–64°F)

Direct
sunlight

Fuchsia spp.
Ladies' eardrops

Hardy and half-hardy fuchsias will brighten any outdoor container display with their intricate, long-lasting blooms. Most are prolific flowerers, with lush green, bronze or variegated foliage. Flower forms may be single, semi-double, or fully double, and colours range from white through shades of pink and red to deepest magenta and purple. *Fuchsia* 'Ballet Girl' grows only 30–47 cm (12–18 in) high and produces large double flowers of cerise and white. Trailing forms such as 'Marinka' are ideal for displaying on a pedestal and will reach 30cm (12in) high with a spread of up to 60cm (24in). Choose a smaller-growing variety for containers of more modest proportions.

Care
Keep the compost moist at all times. Feed with liquid tomato fertilizer at half strength once a week from spring to autumn.

New plants
Take softwood cuttings in spring or semi-ripe cuttings in late summer, and root in seed and cutting compost.

H 15–90cm
(6–36in)
S 45–90cm (18–36in)

16–18°C
(62–64°F)

Partial
shade

Galanthus nivalis

Snowdrop

This hardy winter-flowering clump-forming bulb has pure white, bell-shaped, pendant flowers formed of three larger, outer petals and three, much smaller, green-marked, inner ones. The entirely basal leaves are narrowly strap-shaped and grey-green. Grow in moist but well-drained soil in light sun or partial shade. Propagate by separating clumps or by removing offsets when in leaf. Several variants are grown, including 'Flore Pleno', which has double flowers.

Care
Plant bulbs in the autumn at a depth of three times the height of the bulb. Ensure light sun to partial shade and moist, well-drained soil.

New plants
Lift and divide clumps just after flowering. Replant and allow leaves to die back naturally.

Hyacinthus spp.

Hyacinth

Hardy hyacinths can produce their brightly coloured, highly scented flowers at any time from mid-December to March, according to when they are planted. Bulbs planted before mid-September will flower from mid-December onwards. The most commonly available form is the traditional, single flower-stemmed *Hyacinthus orientalis*. Each flower stem carries up to 40 waxy flowers in colours ranging from pure white through cream, yellow and orange to pink, red, violet and blue over a period of 2–3 weeks. *H.* 'Multiflora White' has multiple stems and white flowers; *H.* 'Jan Bos' has red flowers. It is traditional to grow bulbs in open bowls of fibrous material, but many, particularly hyacinths, will also grow happily in both water and water-retaining gels in a clear- or coloured-glass container.

Care
Keep the compost moist. Once the flowers begin to fade, remove just the flowers and continue watering, leaving the stem and leaves to die down gradually. Work a long-lasting fertilizer into the soil around the bulbs to nourish them as they begin to grow.

New plants
Remove offsets in summer while the bulb is dormant.

H 10cm (4in)
S 10cm (4in)

13–16°C
(55–62°F)

Partial
shade

H 20cm (8in)
S 8cm (3in)

13–16°C
(55–62°F)

Partial
shade

Lantana camara
Yellow sage

Shrub verbena is another name for this strong-smelling, half-hardy tropical perennial, and the tight heads of flowers closely resemble verbena in appearance. It may be grown either as a bushy shrub or trained as a spectacular standard in a container outside for the summer months, as long as it is kept in a warm sheltered place such as a courtyard or an enclosed garden. A packet of seeds will yield plants with red, orange, violet or white flowers that change colour as they age, but there are also named varieties which must be propagated from cuttings.

Care
Yellow sage requires well-drained, light, acidic, soil and a location in direct sunlight. This plant must be overwintered indoors as it will not tolerate low temperatures or frost.

New plants
From seed or cuttings, depending on the variety.

Lilium regale
Regal lily

The lily family is a large one, comprising around 100 bulbous perennial plants. These vary considerably in height, flower size, shape, and colour, but they share certain characteristics. The bulb is always made up of fleshy white or yellow scales, although these may turn purple when exposed to light. Hardy *L. regale* is a fairly all plant for a container, and like other members of the lily family, it grows best in a cool spot, perhaps in a shady corner of a patio or even in a porch. The trumpet-shaped flowers are produced in summer and are white with a yellow throat, heavily scented, and up to 15cm (6in) across.

Care
Keep the compost thoroughly moist at all times as the plant grows and flowers. After flowering, reduce watering to keep the mix just moist as the plant dies down. Fertilize with a high-potash fertilizer every two weeks from when the flower begins to fade until the leaves die down.

New plants
Take healthy scales from the bulb before planting. Remove them cleanly by breaking them from the bulb. Place them in a plastic bag of moist peat-style compost and put in a warm, dark place. Within 6–8 weeks, tiny new bulbils will begin to form on the lower edges of the scales. These can be potted and grown in their own right.

H 100cm (39in)
S 100cm (39in)

16–18°C (62–64°F)

Direct sunlight

H 60cm–2m (2–6ft)

13–16°C (55–62°F)

Partial shade

Osteospermum jucundum
(Dimorphotheca barberae)

Showy, mat-forming half-hardy perennial with lance-shaped, greyish-green leaves. The daisylike flower heads are held well above the leaves in summer. *O. ecklonis* has an erect habit to 60cm (2ft) or more, with white, blue-backed flowers. 'Pink Whirls' has spoon-shaped petals. 'Buttermilk' has yellow florets.

Care
Grow in well-drained soil in full sun. Dead-head plants on a regular basis to ensure continuous flowering.

New plants
Propagate by softwood cuttings in late summer. Winter young plants under glass and plant out in the following spring when frosts are over. Sow seeds under glass in spring.

H 30cm (12in)
S 60cm (24in)

16–18°C
(62–64°F)

Direct
sunlight

Streptosolen jamesonii
Streptosolen

This is a dramatic, slender-stemmed shrub or semivine with elliptic, deep green leaves. The tubular flowers open yellow and turn bright orange and are carried in large, terminal clusters in profusion from spring to summer. Grow in fertile, moist but well-drained soil in sun or partial shade. May be kept to a smaller size by hard pruning after flowering. Propagate by softwood cuttings in early summer.

Care
A good general purpose potting soil (a soil that retains water yet drains well) will suffice for this plant when it is grown in a container. Check purchased soil to see that it is well aerated and add sand or perlite and peat moss if it seems to pack too tightly. This plant must be overwintered indoors as it will not tolerate low temperatures or frost.

New plants
Take stem cuttings in the late spring. It is best to propagate any type of cuttings in a mixture of moist peat and perlite.

Tulipa spp.
Tulip

Tulips are not as easy as some of the other bulbs to grow in containers, but they are well worth attempting. Choose smaller varieties that are labelled for container growing, such as forms of *Tulipa greigii* or *T. kaufmanniana*. Both have a range of flower colours, with both plain and striped petals, and both have attractively marked foliage.

Recommended varieties are *T. kaufmanniana* 'Guiseppe Verdi', which is 15–30 cm (6–12in) high with yellow-and-red striped flowers, and *T. greigii* 'Red Riding Hood', which has red flowers. Greigii hybrids are more robust than many other tulips. The Royal Horticultural Society has given *T. greigii* 'Red Riding Hood' its prestigious Award of Garden Merit (AGM).

Care
Tulips are hardy plants. Keep the compost moist at all times while the plant is in flower, until the leaves turn yellow. Feeding is not necessary.

New plants
Remove offsets from dormant bulbs, and transplant individually.

H 1–2m (3–6ft)

16–18°C (62–64°F)

Direct sunlight

H To 35cm (14in)

13–16°C (55–62°F)

Direct sunlight

Asplenium scolopendrium
Hart's tongue fern

This is a distinctive, evergreen, clump-forming hardy fern with leathery, bright green, strap-shaped fronds which have a heart-shaped base and a pointed tip. Grow in ordinary soil. *A. s.* Crispum Group has boldly crimped leaves. *A. s.* Undulatum Group has less strong undulations.

Care
These plants can be somewhat fussy, so if they will not grow in ordinary soil, try a mix of one part peat, one part coarse sand, one part vermiculite and make sure the mix is lime free. Always use a pot with a hole.

New plants
Propagate by division in early spring.

H To 70cm (28in)
S 60cm (24in)

16–18°C
(62–64°F)

Partial shade

Blechnum gibbum
Miniature tree fern

This is a large fern that will tolerate fairly warm, dry conditions. The fronds are carried in a rosette and can be either sterile or fertile, reaching 90cm (36in) long by 30cm (12in) wide. The shiny green pinnae are slightly drooping. As it grows, a scaly black trunk develops, which can be as tall as 90cm (36in), and gives rise to the common name.

Care
Keep the compost thoroughly moist at all times. Feed with half-strength liquid fertilizer once a month from spring to summer. To maintain adequate humidity, stand the pot on a tray of moist pebbles.

New plants
Detach and transplant offsets if they are produced. Otherwise, it is possible to propagate from spores.

H To 1.2m (4ft)
S 90cm (36in)

16–18°C
(62–64°F)

Partial
shade

Fargesia nitida
Fountain bamboo

This is a pretty, slow-growing hardy bamboo originating from China. It will gradually form a dense thicket of purple-green canes, each marked with powdery white under the leaf nodes. The canes do not branch until they are in their second year of growth, when the upper part of the stems produces a cluster of purple branchlets. Narrow, tapering mid-green leaves are produced in abundance on all stems.

Care
Keep the compost moist at all times. Feed with standard liquid fertilizer once a month during spring to autumn. This is a hardy bamboo in all but the coldest areas.

New plants
Divide clumps of a mature plant, or take cuttings of rhizomes in spring. Root in seed and cutting compost in individual pots.

H 5m (15ft)
S 90cm (36in)

13–16°C
(55–62°F)

Partial
shade

Hakonechloa macra
Golden Japanese forest grass

This is a striking, tufted to mound-forming, hardy herbaceous grass with densely borne, arching, mid- to bright green leaves. Pale green florets are carried in sparse, slender plumes in summer. Grow in ordinary, ideally moist soil in sun or partial shade. Propagate by division in spring. Most commonly seen in gardens in one of its variegated forms, *H. m.* 'Albo-aurea', with leaves striped white and gold, and *H. m.* 'Aureola' with yellow leaves narrowly striped green.

Care
This grass prefers uniformly moist, humus-rich soils and a site in partial shade.

New plants
To propagate, divide in spring.

H 35cm (14in)
S 40cm (16in)

13–16°C
(55–62°F)

Partial
shade

Miscanthus sinensis

Zebra grass

This grass is a handsome, ornamental, clump-forming, herbaceous hardy perennial bearing arching, narrow, matt to slightly bluish-green leaves topped by silk-haired, greyish florets in a sheaf of slender spikes which arch with age. Grow in ordinary, ideally moist soil in sun. Propagate by division in spring. *M. s.* 'Silberfeder' ('Silver Feather') is a reliable, free-flowering cultivar. *M. s.* 'Zebrinus' has broader leaves with zones of white to cream and green.

Care

This plant tolerates some drought and occasional wetness. It prefers soil that is well-drained, loamy, sandy or clay with a pH preference of an acidic to slightly alkaline (6.8–7.7).

New plants

Propagation is from division and seeds in the autumn and spring. Many people prefer to cut the grass back to the ground in the spring so new green growth is not mixed with last year's dried brown foliage.

H 1.5m (5ft)
S 50cm (20in)

13–16°C
(55–62°F)

Direct sunlight

Molinia caerulea

Purple moor grass

This densely tufted, herbaceous hardy perennial has slender, arching, mid-green leaves and erect, yellow-flushed flowering stems bearing loose, narrow heads of tiny, purplish florets. Grow in moist soil in sun or partial shade. Propagate by division in spring.

Care

This grass prefers well-drained to moist soil which is acid to neutral. It prefers direct sunlight but will also tolerate partial shade. Lift and divide congested clumps in autumn or spring. If it is not supported by other plants, use ring stakes or brushwood supports before flowering. Remove old flower heads in spring and comb out dead foliage using a hand fork.

New plants

Divide in spring or autumn. Sow seeds in spring in a cold frame.

H 60cm (24in)
S 30cm (12in)

13–16°C
(55–62°F)

Direct
sunlight

Phyllostachys aurea

Fishpole bamboo, Golden bamboo

This is a colourful, clump-forming hardy bamboo, with stiffly erect, grooved canes which are bright green at first, then brownish yellow. The branchlets bear narrowly lance-shaped, yellowish- to golden-green leaves. Grow in ordinary soil in full sun or partial shade, sheltered from freezing winds. Propagate by division in spring. *P. nigra*, Black Bamboo, has more slender green canes that turn lustrous black in their second or third year.

Care

This plant requires a good general purpose potting soil (a soil that retains water yet drains well). Check purchased soil to see that it is well aerated and add sand or perlite and peat moss if it seems to pack too tightly.

New plants

Division of rhizomes/division in the late winter through spring. After dividing the rhizomes, replant in the plants regular potting mix.

H 2.4m (8ft)
S 3m (10ft)

13–16°C
(55–62°F)

Direct sunlight

Polypodium vulgare
Common polypody

This is an evergreen hardy fern with narrowly triangular to lance-shaped fronds, deeply dissected into bright green lobes. Grow in well-drained soil in indirect sunlight or partial shade. *P. interjectum* is very similar. 'Cornubiense' makes good ground cover.

Care
Grow in humus-rich, moist, but well-drained soil. Bright midday sun can cause damage, and this plant can be sensitive to fungicides. It is able to handle dry shade but water regularly during the first season and mulch the tops of all containers thoroughly.

New plants
Propagate by division in spring or early summer.

H 30cm (12in)
S 90cm (36in)

13–16°C
(55–62°F)

Partial shade

Polystichum setiferum

Holly fern, Shield fern

This is an evergreen, clump-forming hardy fern, with low, arching, lance-shaped fronds dissected into tiny, toothed, oval leaflets. Grow in well-drained soil in partial to full shade. Propagate by division in spring or by detaching plantlets from old fronds. Divisilobum Group includes cultivars with feathery, finely dissected fronds.

Care
Plant in a most cool, moist, lightly shaded site or full sun if given plenty of moisture. Tolerant of dry shade but water regularly in their first season and mulch well.

New plants
Sow spores at 15–16°C (59–61°F) when ripe. Divide rhizomes in spring. Detach fronds bearing bulbils in autumn.

H 60cm (24in)
S 60cm (24in)

13–16°C
(55–62°F)

Partial
shade

Pseudosasa japonica
Arrow bamboo

This is a very hardy bamboo, which eventually forms thickets of erect, olive-green stems which mature to pale brown. The dark green, oblong to lance-shaped leaves are 30cm (12in) or more in length. Grow in moist soil in sun or partial shade. Propagate by division or by separating rooted stems in spring.

Care
This plant requires a good general purpose potting soil (a soil that retains water yet drains well). Check purchased soil to see that it is well aerated and add sand or perlite and peat moss if it seems to pack too tightly.

New plants
Division in the spring. After dividing the plant, pot in the plant's regular potting mix.

H 2.4m (8ft)
S 3m (10ft)

13–16°C
(55–62°F)

Direct
sunlight

Sasa palmata
Palm bamboo

This is a handsome, vigorous half-hardy bamboo which spreads widely by woody rhizomes and bears erect to slightly arching, green canes, sometimes purple-streaked. The large, broadly elliptic leaves are glossy bright rich green with paler midribs. The leaf tips may turn brown in severe winters. Grow in ordinary, preferably moist garden soil in sun or shade. Propagate by division or by separating rooted stems in spring. *S. veitchii* has scarious, parchment-coloured leaves giving the effect of variegation.

Care
Palm bamboo requires a fertile, moisture-retentive soil that does not get waterlogged. It will grow well in most soils including clay. If planting in free-draining soil, water well in the summer. Plant palm bamboo in full sun to part shade away from strong winds.

New plants
Division in the spring. After dividing the plant, pot in the plant's regular potting mix.

Stipa arundinacea
Giant feather grass, Golden oats

This is an elegant, tufted, hardy evergreen which is also known as pheasant grass, producing slender, arching, dark green leaves turning orange-brown in autumn. The large, airy, flowering plumes are formed of many, purplish-green florets. Grow in well-drained soil in sun. Propagate by division in spring. *S. calamagrostis* has bluish-green leaves and smaller, more compact, floral plumes of purple-tinted to buff spikelets. *S. gigantea* is a fine, large specimen grass growing 2m (6ft) or more, with robust, erect stems bearing huge, loose plumes of purplish-green florets which turn corn-yellow when ripe.

Care
Grow in moderately fertile, well-drained soil in full sun. Remove the old foliage in early spring.

New plants
Sow seed in a cold frame in spring; divide from mid-spring to early summer.

H 2.4m (8ft)
S 3m (10ft)

16–18°C
(62–64°F)

Direct
sunlight

H 2m (6ft)
S 3m (10ft)

13–16°C
(55–62°F)

Direct
sunlight

Yushania anceps
Anceps Bamboo

An elegant, colony-forming half-hardy bamboo with glossy dark green canes, erect then arching. The slender branches bear numerous narrowly lance-shaped, mid-green leaves. Grow in ordinary garden soil in sun or partial shade, ideally sheltered from freezing winds. Propagate by division or by separating individual, rooted stems in spring.

Care
Grow in fertile, humus-rich moist but well-drained soil in full sun or partial shade.

New plants
Divide in spring.

H 2.4m (8ft)
S 3m (10ft)

16–18°C
(62–64°F)

Direct
sunlight

Hedera canariensis

Algerian ivy, Canary Island ivy

A vigorous, hardy large-leaved ivy that thrives in cooler locations in a container on a sheltered patio, this is equally useful for climbing, trailing, weaving around posts or as a groundcover in a very large container. The stems and undersides of young leaves are covered with small red hairs, and until the plant reaches its adult phase – when the leaves change shape and texture – they are lobed, thick, matt and leathery. *Hedera canariensis* 'Gloire de Marengo' has leaves that are light green, edged and splashed with creamy white.

Care

Keep the compost moist during spring to autumn. In winter, apply only sufficient water to prevent it drying out. In high temperatures, increase the humidity by misting or standing the pot on a tray of moist pebbles. Feed with standard liquid fertilizer every two weeks from spring to autumn.

New plants

Adventitious roots are produced at leaf nodes along each stem, so propagation can be done by layering or by taking tip cuttings and rooting them in water or potting compost.

H To 4m (12ft)

16–18°C
(62–64°F)

Partial shade

Laurus nobilis

Bay

Ultimately a large evergreen shrub or small tree, this hardy woody plant originates in the Mediterranean. It has aromatic, oval-shaped, glossy mid-green leaves and clusters of small yellow flowers that appear in spring. It can be clipped into a variety of ornamental shapes, and the dried leaves are commonly used in cooking. Although it is often grown in the garden, it also makes a good plant for a conservatory or greenhouse, especially when it is clipped into a formal shape.

Care

Keep moist in spring and summer, and spray the leaves with water occasionally to keep them clean and shining. Keep the plant out of draughts.

New plants

Take a cutting with a heel around 12.5cm (5in) long in early summer. Alternatively, layer established plants in summer. Insert several cuttings in pots of seeds and cutting compost, but transplant individually when the roots are established.

Aeonium arboreum 'Zwartkop'

This is an upright, succulent half-hardy sub-shrub that has long been popular in frost-free areas as a striking plant for an outdoor container. It looks equally impressive in a container on its own or used to contrast with brighter-coloured foliage or flowers. Each basal branch produces a tightly packed rosette of narrow, spoon-shaped leaves, edged with fine hairs. They are a striking dark, glossy, purple-black colour, shading to emerald green at the base, giving each rosette a green centre. Older plants will produce large, pyramid-shaped clusters of yellow flowers in spring, up to 30cm (12in) tall.

Care

Keep the compost moist at all times but not wet, and give standard liquid fertilizer once a month during the growing season. If the plant is kept in too dark a position, the leaves will become more green. In direct sunlight, they may scorch. This plant must be overwintered indoors as it will not tolerate low temperatures or frost.

New plants

Take smaller rosettes as cuttings in early summer. Root in barely damp cactus compost and place in good light.

H 1.5m (5ft)

16–18°C (62–64°F)

Direct sunlight

H 90cm (36in) S 60cm (24in)

16–18°C (62–64°F)

Partial shade

Cordyline australis
Cabbage palm

This is an upright specimen plant that would ultimately form a palm-like, woody stemmed tree if space allowed. The spiky foliage is ideal for adding a focal point to a mixed planting, but it is just as attractive when used alone. The long, strap-like leaves arch outwards from a central tuft or rosette. They can reach 30–90cm (12–36in) long and may be highly coloured or striped. *C. australis* 'Albertii' has matt green leaves with a red central midrib and pink edges, with cream stripes down each leaf. In summer, mature plants produce clusters of tiny creamy white, sweetly scented flowers, sometimes followed by white or bluish-tinted berries.

Care
Keep moist from spring to autumn. In winter, apply sufficient water to prevent compost from drying out. Feed with standard liquid fertilizer monthly from spring to late summer. Cordyline is generally trouble-free, but watch out for scale insects and red spider mites.

New plants
Sow seed at 16°C (60°F) in spring, or alternatively, remove rooting suckers in spring.

H 90cm
(36in)

15–17°C
(60–62°F)

Direct
sunlight

Glossary

Annual A plant that completes its cycle of germination from setting seed through dying in a single growing season.

Biennial A plant requiring two growing seasons to flower and seed.
Bract A leaf at base of flower stalk or flower head.
Bulb A plant storage organ, usually formed underground, containing the following year's growth buds.

Calyx Usually green, outer part of a flower, formed from the sepals, that encases the petals in bud.
Corm A swollen stem base that acts as a storage organ, similar to a bulb.
Crown The part of a herbaceous plant from where new stems are produced.
Cultivar A man-made or cultivated variety, produced by hybridization.
Cutting A section of a plant removed for propagation.

Division The splitting of a plant clump into various sections containing roots and shoots; normally done when the plant is dormant, for purposes of propagating or reinvigorating the plant.
Double flowers Applied to a flower head or bloom having more petals than the original species.

Floret One of the individual flowers that make up the head of a composite flower, such as a dahlia.
Flower head A mass of small flowers that appear as one flower.
Force (-ing) A method of promoting early flowering or fruiting, usually via artificial heat and light.

Half-hardy A plant that withstands low temperatures but not freezing.
Hardy A plant that tolerates year-round conditions in temperate climates, including normal frost, without protection.

Herbaceous A non-woody plant that dies down to its rootstock in winter.
Hybrid A plant resulting from crossing two different species.

Inflorescence A group or arrangement of flowers on a stem, such as panicles and racemes.

Layering A method of pinning a stem to the ground and inducing it to form roots, thereby propagating a separate plant.

Mulch A layer of organic or inorganic material added to the surface of the soil to retain moisture, help suppress weeds and gradually improve fertility.

Node The point at which a leaf grows from the stem.

Offset A plant that is reproduced naturally from the base of the parent plant.

Perennial A plant that lives for longer than two seasons.

Raceme A long, unbranched flower stem.
Rhizome An underground, often creeping, stem acting as a storage organ, from which roots and shoots grow.
Rootball The roots together with the soil adhering to them when a plant is lifted, e.g. for transplanting.

Sepals The green outer parts of a flower, collectively forming the calyx.
Single flowers Applied to a flower that has the normal number of petals for its species, such as a daisy.

Type Used to refer to an original plant species.

Variety A variant of a plant species, arising either naturally or as a result of selection.

Index